D1316824

FLYING

THE GOLDEN YEARS

This absorbing artist's impression of passengers is from the archives of *The illustrated London News.* The cabin environment proved a major step forward in the transition from aeroplanes designed primarily for flying the mail, to those designed primarily for passengers.

FLYING

THE GOLDEN YEARS
A PICTORIAL ANTHOLOGY

Compiled by
Rupert Prior

With a Foreword by
AE Tagg

TIGER BOOKS INTERNATIONAL
LONDON

**For Charles and Phoebe –
infants of the Spring.**

CLB 4045
This 1994 edition published by
Tiger Books International PLC, London
© 1994 CLB Publishing, Godalming, Surrey
All rights reserved
ISBN 1-85501-464-5

Printed and bound in Hong Kong

CONTENTS

FOREWORD

In these days of everyday travel by jet-propelled transport aircraft, with military aircraft and one civilian type, – Concorde, – regularly exceeding supersonic speed, it is easy to take a complacent attitude towards aviation. Flight has developed out of all recognition in the lifetime of most people, from barely controlled hops across the grass airfields to high speed take-offs and landings along concrete runways in most weathers. This has allowed the establishment of a network of airlines flying regular services throughout the world, which is now used by millions of passengers.

The aspiration to fly existed for many centuries, but was not realised until the 18th. century when ballooning began in France and developed there and elsewhere as a sport and entertainment, though one that had, with some limited military use. Its uselessness as a serious means of transport, though, was apparent and directed attention to controllable elongated balloons, known as dirigibles, sustained first by hydrogen gas and later by inert helium, which served for both peaceful and warlike purposes. The name "Zeppelin" became synonymous with the large rigid airship, irrespective of its origin, but the various catastrophes that occurred with their use spelled the end of the large rigids before the outbreak of the second world war.

Nevertheless, lighter-than-air flight, using small non-rigids, had a considerable vogue between 1939 and 1945, and subsequently was taken up by the U.S. Navy for surveillance purposes. Ballooning as a sporting pastime has had something of a revival in recent times, with the development of strong lightweight fabrics for the envelope and lightweight gas burners for providing hot air. Small helium-filled airships have also been revived on a very limited scale, being used mainly for advertising purposes.

It is this heavier-than-air machine, now firmly established for many years, that is the major means of communication and military power in the form of the jet-propelled aircraft with which we are familiar today. These are great technical achievements in themselves, bearing little resemblance to the machines of the early days, but are nevertheless the result of progressive development from the work of the earliest pioneers.

When Wilbur and Orville Wright made four flights on a powered aircraft on the 17th December, 1903, the longest of which was 59 seconds, the brothers had achieved their success after experimentation with models and full-size gliders, their first gliding attempts being made at Kitty Hawk, USA, in 1900. Their bicycle-making experience enabled them to construct their own airframe and, with the help of their employee Charles Taylor, to make a lightweight petrol engine giving sufficient power, albeit with an assisted take-off, to keep the aircraft airborne. Their own experiments and the limited information available on the work of others made them aware of the importance of control in the air, particularly in the lateral plane, which they resolved with the use of wing-walking. This they regarded as their invention, and patented and jealously protected it.

Santos-Dumont, a Brazilian living in Paris, who had constructed and successfully flown eleven airships since 1898, turned his attention to heavier-than-air flight in 1906. In a Voisin-built tail-first biplane on the 12th November, he became the first man to fly in Europe, achieving a distance of 122 metres. His flight lasted just 21 seconds, a height of 6 metres and speed of 41 kms. per hour being recorded. Voisin constructed the machine without lateral control, relying on side curtains between the wings and dihedral to maintain level flight. Unbeknown to most people in Europe was the fact that the Wrights had flown distances of up to 24 miles in over 38 minutes by October 1905. These performances were not equalled, except by later Wright machines, by any other aircraft until 1909.

It was not until 1908 that Wilbur Wright came to France and carried out flights demonstrating his masterly control of the machine. In August

6

he began with brief flights, following in September with one of 1 hour 31 minutes, and culminating on the last day of the year with one of 2 hours 20 minutes. These achievements were marred by an accident to Orville in America, in which he was severely injured and his passenger, Lieut. Selfridge, became the first fatality of powered flight in September 1908. The first pilot aviator to give his life in the cause was Capt. Ferber, who died in a crash at Boulogne on the 7th September 1909, followed later that month by another Frenchman, Eugene Lefebvre. Wilbur's flights far exceeded the efforts of the French aviators, the best of which, Henry Farman, British born but French by adoption, has achieved 20 minutes in July and 45 minutes in October in his Voisin machine. It was apparent that the Wright biplane had superior qualities and that great advances were necessary by European aspirants, if they were to succeed.

This was the spur to greater achievement, particularly in France, where aviation forged ahead, undoubtedly holding the leading position in the period prior to the Great War of 1914-18. At the end of 1911 there 433 licensed aviators in France, compared with 171 in Britain and fewer in the U.S.A. and elsewhere. Tragically, accidents had taken the lives of a further 29 in France and seven in Britain during this year of growth. Some indication of the advances made can be gained from the international records of the years 1909-10-11, all held by French aviators on French machines.

Henry Farman held the record for duration in 1909 with 4 hours 17 minutes, increasing this to 8 hours 12 minutes the following year – but he surrendered his position in 1911 to Fourny who had 11 hours 1 minute. Distance in a closed circuit increased in the same period from 145 miles to 350 and then to 460 miles. The maximum altitude recorded in 1909 was 1,485 feet, increasing to 10,746 feet in 1910 and 13,943 feet in 1911. Accurate means of recording ultimate speeds had not been established but 45 m.p.h.

was representative for 1909, with estimates of 80 m.p.h. for the fastest Blériot in 1910 and 90 m.p.h. for a 1911 Nieuport.

Progress in design resulted in many varied configurations from monoplanes to quadruplanes, both pusher and tractor types, and some early attempts with rotary wings. Conflict over the Wright patents dragged on for some years but was eventually resolved. Control systems were improved and generally moving towards standardisation with wing warping eventually to give way to ailerons operated by stick or wheel and elevators by fore and aft movement of the control column, with the rudder operated by foot pedals.

Britain got off to a slow start with little encouragement from the government, who initiated work at Farnborough, but abandoned that carried out by Cody and Dunne on separate projects on financial grounds and lack of foresight for future applications in support of the military. It took the crossing of the Channel by Blériot in July 1909, in a monoplane of his own creation, and the performances at Reims in September at the world's first great aviation meeting to cause a rethink of policy and for British firms and individuals to commence operations. Initially much use was made of French machines, mainly Blériot, Voisin and Farman, and Moore-Brabazon, who was the first Englishman to achieve a circular flight of one mile, earning himself the *Daily Mail* Prize of L1,000 and the first official British pilots licence, carried out his early flying on Voisins, but it was an early Short biplane on which he was successful. Although the first Short machine exhibited at the Aero Show at Olympia in March 1909 was abandoned, the firm, after producing six Wright biplanes under licence, soon produced successful machines to their own designs. These owed much to the Wright and later the Farmer pusher biplanes, the latter itself derived from Voisin's boxkite biplanes, but incorporating ailerons for lateral control.

7

The years from 1910 were ones of great hopes in aviation and steady progress was made in Europe, America and to a lesser degree in other parts of the world. In Britain Cody and A.V. Roe were pilots and constructors who contributed greatly to the development of flight. Sopwith and Grahame-White, after succeeding as competition pilots, set up training establishments and entered the field of construction, being joined by others as the need for aircraft for war purposes encouraged the growth of the industry. Grahame-White opened Hendon aerodrome as a major attraction with many flying meetings to bring the art to the attention of the general public. Inevitably some of the flying at meetings was foolhardy and resulted in accidents. These, and accidents to military aircraft in particular, attracted press and parliamentary criticism and it became evident that the failure of the aircraft itself was a major factor requiring a more scientific approach to its design and construction. In France, at Chalais Meudon, the French Government had an establishment for basic research and similar facilities were developed at Farnborough in Britain. The Royal Aircraft Factory, renamed later the Royal Aircraft Establishment, evolved from the old Balloon Factory and, manned by technical and scientific personnel, it developed procedures and standards for the general benefit of the industry. It was inevitable that this work led to the construction of prototype aircraft, in the early days by the improvement and reconstruction of the small number of aircraft purchased by the government for military purposes. The industry was slow to become established and inevitably prototypes from Farnborough were followed by production in some numbers, to the annoyance of the "trade", which the industry, supported by the press, regarded as to their detriment. In truth there were few types of reliable aircraft with military potential available from any source; nevertheless, the army recognised the useful-

ness of aircraft for reconnaissance purposes. At the Factory the approach had been to provide a stable aeroplane for this purpose, requiring the minimum attention to control by the pilot, and this had resulted in the B.E.2 for which Geoffrey de Havilland was responsible for the design and much of the testing. The aircraft had been drawn in some detail and the drawings could be supplied to firms for tendering purposes, so alongside the production at Farnborough a number of firms produced the B.E.2 and this helped to get them established as the nucleus of the industry which was later needed to produce the many thousands of aircraft for operation between 1914-18.

Despite original intentions for a unified air service, the Royal Flying Corps and Royal Navy Air Service had developed separately, but amalgamation was decreed and the Royal Air Force was formed in April 1918. The triumphs and disasters of the airmen of the combatant nations have been extensively documented and must be left to others to do them justice. Suffice it to note that the R.A.F. emerged from the war as a major force with 297,000 men and 22,650 aircraft but was to become a shadow of its former self within a few years of the Armistice. The same was to happen to the industry, which had manufactured over 55,000 aircraft and 41,000 engines. The stimulus of war brought great improvements in aircraft design and performance, but of aircraft specifically for war purposes, so the advent of peace created new problems. The masses of aircraft produced for military purposes were mostly unsuitable for civilian use and large numbers were scrapped as the R.A.F. was run down. Some of the large machines, such as the Handley Page 0/400 could, with small modifications, be used for transport purposes, and a network of lines to Europe was contemplated. Some of the single engined machines such as the D.H.4s and D.H.9s and Bristol Fighters were made acceptable by the

8

addition of enclosures for the passengers and the Avro 504 of pre-war origin continued to find uses as a trainer and for joy-riding purposes. The single seaters found few applications except for some activities by ex-service pilots.

Before the war aviation had been stimulated by cash prizes often put up for competition by large organisations of which the *Daily Mail* was prominent. This was to be repeated after the war with the reinstatement of the £10,000 prize for a successful non-stop crossing of the Atlantic. U.S. Navy airmen accomplished a crossing by flying boat in stages over a period of three weeks, but this was not eligible for the contest. Of several British contenders the Martinsyde, Sopwith and Vickers teams gathered in New-foundland for west to east attempts. Raynham, on the Martinsyde, failed to get airborne twice and Hawker, on the Sopwith Atlantic, came down in the ocean half-way across and was miraculously saved. It was the Vickers Vimy of Alcock and Brown that finally triumphed when it alighted in Ireland with its nose embedded in soft ground. There were many other attempts to cross from both directions, notably that of Lindbergh from mainland America to France, but many lives were lost before reliable aircraft could make the crossing a certainty. Long distance flights to all parts of the world were sponsored for a variety of reasons, the most important being the need to establish routes and gain experience for the regular operation of commercial airlines for the carriage of passengers and mails. Britain eventually chose flying boats for the Empire routes, as did America for its South American and cross-Pacific operations. Internal airlines in Europe and America encouraged the development of more modern landplanes with retractable undercarriages of which the Douglas D.C.3 was the outstanding example.

British companies had their successes in the light aircraft field, particularly with the D.H. Moth and its derivatives, including the Dragon and Rapide employed by the small independent operators who developed internal services until amalgamation and eventual unification took place.

Alongside the growth of civil aviation, the R.A.F., which had been drastically reduced in size in 1919, was allowed to expand to meet commitments in the Middle East, India and Africa. For a decade after the war the aircraft employed were little improved in performance and, indeed, consisted in many cases of wartime types suitably modified. The 1930s saw the introduction into service of the first 200 m.p.h. fighter in the shape of the Fury, which served alongside much larger numbers of two-seater Hawkers and other types which equipped the light bombing and army co-operation squadrons, and their equivalent carrier-based types which equipped the revived Fleet Air Arm. The threat of war caused further reappraisal of Britain's defences, resulting in plans to expand the R.A.F. and the industry that supplied it. Specifications were issued for more advanced types for all classes of operations, which included requirements for a 300 m.p.h. fighter equipped with eight machine guns – this resulted in the Hurricane and Spitfire, both powered by the outstanding Rolls-Royce Merlin engine.

However, quietly working in makeshift premises with a small team, Frank Whittle, an R.A.F. officer, was constructing and testing his first gas turbine engine – a project he had begun as a young officer in 1930. Whilst this new source of power was to play little part in the future hostilities, it subsequently displaced the high-powered piston engine for most military and civil purposes. It has, of course, caused a revolution affecting the lives of everybody for both good and ill and constitutes a major milestone in the years of aviation.

AE Tagg

9

A decorative and dramatic flying-related advertisement. The year 1865 saw the first mature design for a jet-propelled engine, by the French engineer Charles de Louvrié.

IN AT THE START

"High spirits they had:
gravity they flouted"

Cecil Day Lewis

In the beginning - the original Wright aeroplane as presented to the Smithsonian Institute. Orville and Wilbur Wright's success was based on a period of solid achievement in gliding. Their first powered flight in 1903 was made only 4½ years after the brothers had written to the Smithsonian asking for books on flying.

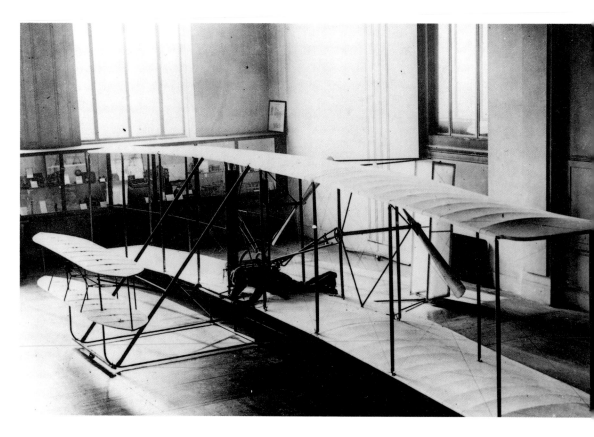

I may be expediting the attainment of an object that will in time be found of great importance to mankind; so much so, that a new era in society will commence from the moment that aerial navigation is familiarly realised. . . . . I feel perfectly confident, however, that this noble art will soon be brought home to man's convenience, and that we shall be able to transport ourselves and our families, and their goods and chattels, more securely by air than by water, and with a velocity of from 20 to 100 miles per hour.

SIR GEORGE CAYLEY (1809)

Well, gentlemen, do you believe in the possibility of aerial locomotion by machines heavier than air? . . . You ask yourselves doubtless if this apparatus, so marvellously adapted for aerial locomotion, is susceptible of receiving greater speed. It is not worth while to conquer space if we cannot devour it. I wanted the air to be a solid support to me, and it is. I saw that to struggle against the wind I must be stronger than the wind, and I am. I had no need of sails to drive me, nor oars nor wheels to push me, nor rails to give me a faster road. Air is what I wanted, that was all. Air surrounds me as water surrounds the submarine boat, and in it my propellers act like the screws of a steamer. That is how I solved the problem of aviation. That is what a balloon will never do, nor will any machine that is lighter than air.

JULES VERNE (1886)

It is therefore incontestably the Wright brothers alone who resolved, in its entirety, the problem of human mechanical flight. . . . . This resulted from their tests from 1903 to 1905. Men of genius – erudite, exact in their reasoning, hard workers, outstanding experimenters, and unselfish – the brothers Wilbur and Orville Wright have, more than anyone else, deserved the success which they achieved. They changed the face of the globe.

CHARLES DOLLFUS
Curator Musée de l'Air, Paris

But we must admit the possibility that continued investigation and experience will bring us ever nearer to that solemn moment, when the first man will rise from earth by means of wings, if

12

only for a few seconds, and marks that historical moment which heralds the inauguration of a new era in our civilization.

OTTO LILIENTHAL (1891)

I believe that simple flight at least is possible to man and that the experiments and investigations of a large number of independent workers will result in the accumulation of information and knowledge and skill which will finally lead to accomplished flight.

WILBUR WRIGHT (1899)

For some years I have been afflicted with the belief that flight is possible to man. My disease has increased in severity and I feel that it will soon cost me an increased amount of money if not my life. What is chiefly needed is skill rather than machinery.

WILBUR WRIGHT (1900)

We are in an uproar getting Will off. The trip will do him good. I don't think he will be reckless.

KATHARINE WRIGHT
(to her father concerning Wilbur in 1900)

There are only two ways of learning to ride a fractious horse: one is to get on him and learn by actual practice how each motion and trick may be best met; the other is to sit on a fence and watch the beast awhile, and then retire to the house and at leisure figure out the best way of overcoming his jumps and kicks. The latter system is the safer, but the former, on the whole, turns out the larger proportion of good riders. It is very much the same in learning to ride a flying machine; if you are looking for perfect safety you will do well to sit on a fence and watch the birds, but if you really wish to learn you must mount a machine and become acquainted with its tricks by actual trial.

WILBUR WRIGHT (1901)

During the night of 16th December 1903, a strong cold wind blew from the north. When we rose on the morning of the 17th, the puddles of water, which had been standing about camp since the recent rains, were covered with ice. The wind had a velocity of 22 to 27 m.p.h. We thought it would die down before long, but when 10 o'clock arrived, and the wind was as brisk as ever, we decided that we had better get the machine out. . . . Wilbur having used his turn in the unsuccessful attempt on the 14th, the right to the first trial belonged to me. Wilbur ran at the side, holding the wings to balance it on the track. The machine, facing a 27-mile wind, started very slowly. Wilbur was able to stay with it until it lifted ponderously from the track after a forty-foot run.

The course of the flight up and down was exceedingly erratic. The control of the front rudder was difficult. As a result, the machine would rise suddenly to about ten feet, and then as suddenly dart for the ground. A sudden dart when a little over 120 feet from the point at which it rose into the air, ended the flight.

This flight lasted only twelve seconds, but it was nevertheless the first in the history of the world in which a machine carrying a man had raised itself by its own power into the air in full flight, had sailed forward without reduction of speed, and had finally landed at a point as high as that from which it started.

ORVILLE WRIGHT (1903)

Paris 1908 and spectators watch Henri Farman, former artist turned racing cyclist and driver, who had built his first glider in 1907, testing it on the sands at Le Touquet. Most successful of European pilots, Farman had a far-reaching influence on the development of aviation.

13

LEARNINGS IN BEE CULTURE
Eye Witness account published in 1905

Dear friends, I have a wonderful story to tell you – a story that, in some respects, outrivals the Arabian Nights fables – a story, too, with a moral that I think many of the younger ones need, and perhaps some of the older ones too if they will heed it. God in his great mercy has permitted me to be, at least somewhat, instrumental in ushering in and introducing to the great wide world an invention that may outrank electric cars, the automobiles, and all other methods of travel, and one which may fairly take a place beside the telephone and wireless telegraphy. Am I claiming a good deal? Well, I will tell my story, and you shall be the judge. In order to make the story a helpful one I may stop and turn aside a good many times to point a moral.

In our issue for Sept. 1, I told you of two young men, two farmer's boys, who love machinery, down in the central part of Ohio. I am now going to tell you something of two other boys, a minister's boys, who love machinery, and who are interested in the modern developments of science and art. Their names are Orville and Wilbur Wright, of Dayton, Ohio. I made mention of them and their work on page 241 of our issue of March 1 last. You may remember it. These two, perhaps by accident, or may be as a matter of taste, began studying the flights of birds and insects. From this they turned their attention to what has been done in the way of enabling men to fly. They not only studied nature, but they procured the best books, and I think I may say all the papers, the world contains on this subject. When I first became acquainted with them, and expressed a wish to read up all there was on the subject, they showed me a library that astonished me; and I soon found they were thoroughly versed, not only in regard to our present knowledge, but every thing that had been done in the past. The boys (they are men now), instead of spending

Claude Grahame-White (1879-1959), a remarkable and natural pilot, had founded his own aviation company by 1911 when these finishing touches were made for the first aerial post from Hendon. Grahame-White later turned the field into the famous between-the- wars aerodrome.

their summer vacation with crowds and with such crowds as are often questionable, as so many do, went away by themselves to a desert place by the seacoast. You and I have in years past found enjoyment and health in sliding down hill on the snow; but these boys went off to that sandy waste on the Atlantic coast to slide down hill too; but instead of sliding on snow and ice they slid on air. With a gliding machine made of sticks and cloth they learned to glide and soar from the top of a hill to the bottom; and by making not only hundreds but more than a thousand experiments, they became so proficient in gliding these machines that they could sail like a bird, and control its movements up and down as well as sideways. Now this was not altogether for fun or boys' play.[1]* They had a purpose in view. I want to stop right here to draw one of my morals. If I allude to myself somewhat, please do not think I do it because I wish to boast. Some of you have read or heard me tell of the time when my attention was first called to bees. Almost the first thing I did was to go to the bookstores and see what books were

to be found on the subject. I studied these books day and night, and read them over and over again. Then I procured the books and bee-journals from the old world; and when the language was something I could not manage I hired an interpreter to translate for me until I knew pretty nearly what the book contained. In less than one year I was in touch with the progressive bee-keepers of the world; and the American Bee Journal, that had been dropped for lack of support, was started up again. I mention this to show you that my success in bee culture, from the very first, was not luck or chance. It was the result of untiring energy and work. Now let me draw a contrast. During the years that are past, quite a number of men have come to me with their patented hives. A good many of these men had never seen a bee-journal. Some of them who had paid out their hard earnings to the Patent Office had almost never seen a book on bee culture, and they were not sure, from actual experience, of the existence of the queen-bee. We have inventors at the present time who are giving their lives and money to the four winds in the same poor foolish way. If you wish to make a success of anything, or in any line among the many lines that lie before us in this great world of ours, find out what the great and good men have done in this special line before you.

Well, these two men spent several summers in that wild place, secure from intrusion, with their gliding machine. When they became experts they brought in, as they had planned to do, a gasoline engine to furnish power, and made a

Knight of the air and pioneer demonstration pilot Alan Cobham flew to every major centre in Britain in an effort to encourage the building of municipal airports. His aerial circus visited 300 towns every year. He was knighted in 1926.

Public enthusiasm for flying was well-reflected in such static displays as the Paris Salon and the Olympia Show. Here is a general view of the Olympia exhibits in 1914.

15

The beat of the wind and the roar of the engine - a flight home through oncoming dusk? One of the new flying machines remains convincingly aloft in an Edwardian study.

The Curtiss Reims machine won the newly presented Gordon Bennett Trophy for the fastest speed over a course of 20 kilometres in 1909.

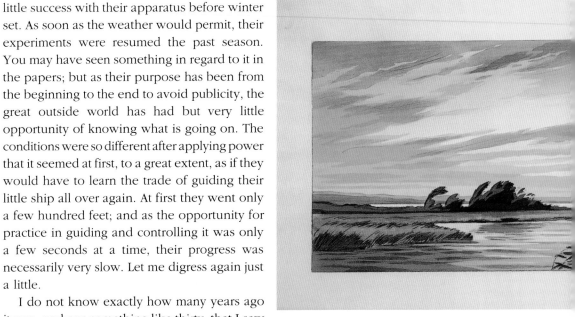

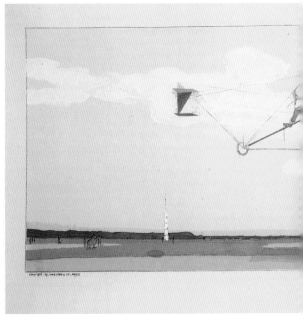

little success with their apparatus before winter set. As soon as the weather would permit, their experiments were resumed the past season. You may have seen something in regard to it in the papers; but as their purpose has been from the beginning to the end to avoid publicity, the great outside world has had but very little opportunity of knowing what is going on. The conditions were so different after applying power that it seemed at first, to a great extent, as if they would have to learn the trade of guiding their little ship all over again. At first they went only a few hundred feet; and as the opportunity for practice in guiding and controlling it was only a few seconds at a time, their progress was necessarily very slow. Let me digress again just a little.

I do not know exactly how many years ago it was, perhaps something like thirty, that I saw in the Scientific American that they had in France what was called at that time a veloci-pede. As soon as I saw the description I sent an order for one, and I think I had about the first machine in the semblance of a bicycle that was ever in Ohio – perhaps one of the first brought into the United States. The machine cost over $100; and as it was a heavy affair, the express on it cost quite an item more. When it came to hand, after days and weeks of anxious waiting, neither myself nor anybody else could ride it at all. The whole town jeered at me, and the story of the "fool and his money" was hurled in my teeth so many times I almost dread to hear it even yet. Men of good fair understanding pointed their fingers at me, and said that anybody of good common sense ought to know that, that thing would not stand up with a man on it, for that would be an utter impossibility. I worked at it, the crowd in my way, for several hours in the morning. Finally I rented the largest hall in the town, went in with one trusty boy who had faith, for a companion, and locked the door. After quite a little practice on the smooth floor of the hall I succeeded in riding from one end to the other; but I could not turn the corners. When, after still more practice, I did turn one corner without falling, how my spirits arose! A little later I went in a wabbly way clear around the room. Then my companion did the same thing,

and, oh how we did rejoice and gather faith! A little later on, with a flushed but happy face, I went out into the street and rode around the public square. You can guess the rest of it. Well, these boys wanted just the same kind of privacy to try their flying-machine that I needed for my velocipede; but as it measures about forty feet from the tip of one wing to the tip of the other, instead of a large hall they wanted a large level field in some out-of-the-way place. I found them in a pasture lot of 87 acres, a little over half a mile long and nearly as broad. The few people who occasionally got a glimpse of the experiments, evidently considered it only another Darius Green but I recognized at once they were really scientific explorers who were serving the world in much the same way that Columbus did when he discovered America, and just the same way that Edison, Marconi, and a host of others have done all along through the ages.

In running an automobile or a bicycle you have to manage the steering only to the right and left; but an air-ship has to be steered up and down also. When I first saw the apparatus it persisted in going up and down like the waves of the sea. Sometimes it would dig its nose in the dirt, almost in spite of the engineer. After repeated experiments it was finally cured of its foolish tricks, and was made to go like a steady old horse. This work, mind you, was all new. Nobody living could give them any advice. It was like exploring a new and unknown domain. Shall I tell you how they cured it of bobbing up and down? Simply by loading its nose or front steering apparatus with cast iron. In my ignorance I thought the engine was not large enough; but when fifty pounds of iron was fastened to the "nose" (as I will persist in calling it), it came down to a tolerably straight line and carried the burden with ease. There was a reason for this that I can not explain here. Other experiments had to be made in turning from right to left; and, to make the matter short, it was my privilege, on the 20th day of September, 1904, to see the first successful trip of an airship, without a balloon to sustain it, that the world has ever made, that is, to turn the corners and come back to the starting point. During all of these experiments they have kept so near the soft marshy ground

On water - Meeting de Tamise, 1912. The first flight by a float plane was made by Fabre in 1910 and, by 1912, the seaplane had come properly into its own.

17

One of history's classic aeroplanes: Farman's Henri Farman III, a vivid image in a vivid landscape from 1909. A well-dressed well-wisher helps to set the scene.

Ernest Montaut's spirited designs and posters were highly decorative, dramatic and very much in the spirit of the age. *Un Match Moderne,* **a lithograph dating from 1907, depicts a race between a Renault G.P. car and a pusher biplane.**

18

that a fall would be no serious accident, either to the machine or its occupant. In fact, so carefully have they managed, that, during these years of experimenting, nothing has happened to do any serious damage to the machine nor to give the boys more than what might be called a severe scratch. I think great praise is due to them along this very line. They have been prudent and cautious. I told you there was not another machine equal to such a task as I have mentioned, on the face of the earth; and, furthermore, just now as I dictate there is probably not another man besides these two who has learned the trick of controlling it. In making this last trip of rounding the circle, the machine was kept near the ground, except in making the turns. If

By the 20th cen-
tury, all the various
aesthetic potentiali-
ties of bronze had
been developed - as
revealed in this
somewhat fanciful
early English flying
sculpture.

you will watch a large bird when it swings around in a circle you will see its wings are tipped up at an incline. This machine must follow the same rule; and to clear the tip of the inside wing it was found necessary to rise to a height of perhaps 20 or 25 feet. When the engine is shut off the apparatus glides to the ground very quietly, and alights on something much like a pair of light sled-runners, sliding over the grassy surface perhaps a rod or more. Whenever it is necessary to slow up the speed before alighting, you turn the nose up hill. It will then climb right up on the air until the momentum is exhausted, when, by skilful management, it can be dropped as lightly as a feather.

Since the above was written they have twice succeeded in making four complete circles without alighting, each circle passing the starting point. These circles are nearly a mile in circumference each and the last flight made, Dec. 1, could have been prolonged indefinitely had it not been that the rudder was in such position it cramped the hand of the operator so he was obliged to alight. The longest flight took only five minutes and four seconds by the watch. Over one hundred flights have been made during the past summer. Some of them reached perhaps 50 or 60 feet above ground. On both these long trips seventy pounds instead of fifty of cast iron was carried on the "nose."

Everybody is ready to say, "Well, what use is it? What good will it do?" These are questions no

The dawn - Wright's Flyer I makes the first powered, sustained and controlled aeroplane flight in history, with Orville piloting, at Kill Devil Hills, near Kitty Hawk, U.S.A., on the morning of December 17, 1903. "The age of the flying machine has come at last", said Orville.

man can answer as yet. However, I will give you a suggestion or two. The man who made this last trip said there was no difficulty whatever in going above the trees or anywhere he chose; but perhaps wisdom would dictate he should have still more experience a little nearer the ground. The machine easily made thirty or forty miles an hour, and this in going only a little more than half a mile straight ahead. No doubt it would get up a greater speed if allowed to do so perhaps, with the wind, a mile a minute after the first mile. The manager could doubtless go outside of the field and bring it back safely, to be put in the little house where it is kept nights. But no matter how much time it takes, I am sure all the world will commend the policy so far pursued – go slowly and carefully, and avoid any risk that might cause the loss of a human life. This great progressive world can not afford to take the risk of losing the life of either of these two men.[2*]

I have suggested before, friends, that the time may be near at hand when we shall not need to fuss with good roads nor railway tracks, bridges, etc., at such an enormous expense. With these machines we can bid adieu to all these things. God's free air, that extends all over the earth, and perhaps miles above us, is our training field.

Rubber tires, and the price of rubber, are no longer "in it." The thousand and one parts of the automobile that go to make its construction, and to give it strength, can all be dispensed with. You can set your basket of eggs almost anywhere on the upper or lower deck, they will not even rattle unless it be when they come to alight.

There are hundreds of queer things coming to light in regard to this new method of travel; and I confess it is not clear to me, even yet, how that little aluminium engine, with four paddles, does the work. I asked the question, "Boys, would that engine and these two propellers raise the machine from the ground if placed horizontally above it?"

"Certainly not, Mr. Root. They would not lift a quarter of its weight."

"Then how is it possible that it sustains it in the air as it is?"

The answer involves a strange point in the wonderful discovery of air navigation. When some large bird or butterfly is soaring with motionless wings, a very little power from behind will keep it moving. Well, if this motion is kept up, a very little incline of the wings will keep it from falling. A little more incline, and a little more push from behind, and the bird or the

Wilbur Wright. The Wright brothers success marked the real birth of the aeroplane. Enthusiasm for both the designer and constructor of aircraft followed their achievements and a small group of aeronautical pioneers collectively built an industry from nothing in the early years.

butterfly, or the machine created by human hands, will gradually rise in the air. I was surprised at the speed, and I was astonished at the wonderful lifting power of this comparatively small apparatus. When I saw it pick up the fifty pounds of iron so readily I asked if I might ride in place of the iron. I received, by way of assurance, the answer that the machine would no doubt carry me easily. You see then I would have the "front seat"; and even if it is customary (or used to be in olden times) to accord the front seat to the ladies, I think the greater part of them would say, "Oh! Sit still, Mr. Root. Do not think of getting up to give us your seat."

At first there was considerable trouble about getting the machine up in the air and the engine well up to speed. They did this by running along a single rail track perhaps 200 feet long. It was also, in the early experiments, found advisable to run against the wind, because they could then have a greater time to practice in the air and not get so far away from the building where it was stored. Since they can come around to the starting point, however, they can start with the wind even behind them; and with a strong wind behind it is an easy matter to make even more than a mile a minute. The operator takes his place lying flat on his face. This position offers

less resistance to the wind. The engine is started and got up to speed. The machine is held until ready to start by a sort of trap to be sprung when all is ready; then with a tremendous flapping and snapping of the four cylinder engine, the huge machine springs aloft. When it first turned that circle, and came near the starting point, I was right in front it; and I said then, and I believe still, it was one of the grandest sights, if not the grandest sight, of my life. Imagine a locomotive that has left its track, and is climbing up in the air right toward you – a locomotive without any wheels, we will say, but with white wings instead, we will further say – a locomotive made of aluminium. Well, now, imagine this white locomotive, with wings that spread 20 feet each way, coming right toward you with a tremendous flap of its propellers, and you will have something like what I saw. The younger brother bade me move to one side for fear it might come down suddenly; but I tell you, friends, the sensation that one feels in such a crisis is something hard to describe. The attendant at one time, when the rope came off that started it, said he was shaking from head to foot as if he had a fit of ague. His shaking was uncalled for, however, for the intrepid manager succeeded in righting up his craft, and she made one of her

A *Daily Mirror* photograph of Robert Loraine equipped for a long over-sea flight, wearing a life belt and with compass and map strapped to his knees.

very best flights. I may add, however, that the apparatus is secured by patents, both in this and in foreign countries; and as nobody else has yet succeeded in doing anything like what they have done I hope no millionaire or syndicate will try to rob them of the invention or laurels they have so fairly and honestly earned.

When Columbus discovered America he did not know what the outcome would be, and no one at that time knew; and I doubt if the wildest enthusiast caught a glimpse of what really did come from his discovery. In a like manner these two brothers have probably not even a faint glimpse of what their discovery is going to bring to the children of men. No one living can give a guess of what is coming along this line, much better than any one living could conjecture the final outcome of Columbus' experiment when he pushed off through the trackless waters. Possibly we may be able to fly over the north pole, even if we should not succeed in tacking the "stars and stripes" to its uppermost end.

Alberto Santos-Dumont (1873-1932), the Paris-based Brazilian who piloted a dirigible round the Eiffel Tower in 1901, and his *14-bis* that made the first hop-flights in Europe in 1906.

1*When I suggested that, even though sliding down hill on the air was very nice, it must have been quite a task to carry the machine back to the top of the hill every time, the reply was something like this:
"Oh! No, Mr. Root – no task at all. Just remember that we always sail against the wind: and by a little shifting of the position, the wind does the greater part of the work in carrying it back." It just blows it back (whenever the wind is strong enough) up hill to the starting point.

2* If these two men should be taken away by accident or otherwise, there is probably no one living who could manage the machine. With these men to teach them "the trade", however, there are plenty who could doubtless learn it in a few weeks.

Success four flights Thursday morning all against twentyone mile wind started from level with engine power alone average speed through air

thirtyone miles longest 57 seconds inform Press home Christmas.

OREVELLE WRIGHT.
(The telegram as received by his father, dated December 17th 1903)
* Through errors in transmission '57' appeared for '59' and 'Orevelle' for 'Orville"

It is not extravagant to say that the 17th of December 1903, when the Wright brothers made the first free flight through the air in a power driven machine, marks the beginning of a new era in the history of the world.
SIR WALTER RALEIGH (1922)

The ground was very rough and hard, and as we tore along, at an increasing pace that was very soon greater than any motor I had yet been in, I expected to be jerked and jolted. But the motion was wonderfully smooth – smoother yet – and then – ! Suddenly there had come into it a new, indescribable quality – a lift – a lightness – a life! Very many there are now who know that feeling: that glorious, gliding sense that the sea-bird has known this million years, and which man so long and so vainly envied it, and which even now, familiarity can never rob of its charm. But picture, if you can, what it meant for the first time; when all the world of Aviation was young and fresh and untried; when to rise at all was a glorious adventure, and to find one self flying swiftly in the air, the too-good-to-be-true realisation of a life long dream. You wonderful aerial record breakers of today and of the years to come, whose exploits I may only marvel at and envy, I have experienced something that can never be yours and can never be taken away from me – the rapture, the glory and the glamour of "the very beginning".

GERTRUDE BACON
(writing of her flight With R. Sommer in 1909)

I know of only one bird – the parrot – that talks; and it can't fly very high.
WILBUR WRIGHT
(in declining to make a speech in 1908)

Gilmour leaves the Brooklands motor course in Surrey, the "cradle" of speed, for Brighton. Flying schools were flourishing by the time this photograph was taken in 1911, with six in operation at the Weybridge track. The famous Blue Bird restaurant is to the right of the picture; it was owned by Eardley Billing, the brother of the eccentric Pemberton Billing MP, who founded the Supermarine Aviation works in in 1913 and was later linked with Vickers at Brooklands. He was the originator of Supermarine Schneider racers, Southampton flying boats and the Spitfire. Pioneer A.V. Roe wrote of the Blue Bird "few places can have seen such visions and dreams created under the sign 'Refreshments at Popular Prices'".

Claude Grahame-White taking off from a street in front of the White House, in Washington, U.S.A. His exhibitionism was greeted enthusiastically by President Taft.

"M. Bellamy's Weird Boat – Humours of the First Cruise"
The Daily Mail, 1907

"Aeroplane at Weybridge – a Great White Bird"
The Daily Mail, 1907

It consists of two attenuated punts on which are fixed the wheels and frame of a motor car. Above this, again, is a 50 h.p. motor driving a propeller about five feet in diameter. It is a weird, top heavy looking structure, but M. Bellamy expressed his confidence yesterday that it would work. The steering apparatus was the crudest imaginable, practically two untrimmed branches of fir tree, with a short plank nailed across. There was a plank nailed across the two punts to stand on, and M. Bellamy managed the motor from a wooden trellis in front.

Blériot did not get up in any blare of trumpets. In the cold, grey dawn of the morning, before the sun had warmed up things, before it had dissipated the dew-drops, he was in our country. It marks a new era in the world.

LIEUTENANT SHACKLETON
(in the Daily Mail, 1909)

The machine, which was set up on a sandy stretch of the motor track, resembles a great white bird. The engine, fixed in a light wooden frame, may be regarded as the body of the bird.

On each side is a cap like structure formed of bamboo rods, the top being covered with white calico. Attached to the engine at the back is a tail of bamboo and white calico – it is ten yards long and four yards wide. The attachment is effected by the means of hinges which will permit the tail to rise and fall as the machine moves through the air.

In front the head of the bird is represented by a contrivance of bamboo and canvas not unlike the feathers of an arrow, its size being proportionate to the other parts of the machine. This is fixed to the engine frame by a swivel, and may be raised or lowered, or turned to the right or to the left at will, and therefore is the means by which M. Bellamy hopes to guide the aeroplane in its flight.

A Voisin boxkite with 50 hp Antoinette engine. Gabriel Voisin, an architectural student who graduated to engineering was responsible with his brother Charles for setting up the first aircraft factory at Billancourt in France in 1905.

25

Flamboyant expatriate - once described as one of the valuable "curiosities" of aviation, American Samuel Franklin Cody was often mistaken for "Buffalo Bill",to whom he was not, however, related. He came to England in 1896 and experimented with man-lifting kites; later, thought he could neither read nor write, Cody taught himself to fly.

FROM THE TIMES
T.O.M. Sopwith, 1910

I had nothing to direct myself by, so I just kept flying on. Towns and villages passed below; I knew none of their names. Then the wind began to get more gusty. The machine swayed and lurched and the arm with which I moved the controlling lever began to ache.

Just as I was flying over a village at about 800 feet a very ugly gust caught my machine on one side and tilted it partly over. To my consternation the aeroplane refused to regain its normal position even when I exerted the full pressure of the small balancing planes fixed to the rear ends of the main planes. It was a moment I am not likely to forget. Changing hands quickly on my steering lever I leaned over as far as I could from my driving seat so as to be able to throw the weight of my body against the rising wing of my machine. Just when I thought I should slide hopelessly down through the air the machine slowly righted itself, but another gust assailed me and I had to look out for a landing place, although I had 11 gallons of petrol left in my tanks and the engine had not misfired once. I was getting frightened. A field near a village presented itself. I planed down and sat still quite exhausted and drained.

Victory for Sopwith and for Britain. Tommy Sopwith's floatplane version of the 100 hp Gnome-engined Sopwith Tabloid won the Schneider Trophy air race at Monaco in 1914. It was piloted by Howard Pixton, who averaged 86.78 mph.

The Sopwith entry for the 1919 Schneider Trophy race. Held off the coast at Bournemouth, the contest proved something of a damp squib and was abandoned due to fog. Jacques Schneider, invalid son of a French armaments baron, first presented the trophy for competition in 1912 to encourage the development of long- range ocean sea-planes.

War Office Blériot monoplane, used by four squadrons, saw service in France in 1914. Military aviation was an essential for the leading European nations and Britain's Royal Flying Corps was formed on April 13, 1912 with the Central Flying School being established at Netheravon, Wiltshire.

FROM THE LONDON MORNING POST
1908

Cody had covered about 500 yards and was 20 feet high before he realised there were trees in the line of flight. He attempted to turn sharply left, but stalled and the tilt became more and more acute until the machine crashed. After the dust had settled and the reporters had run up to him, the undefeatable Cody brazened it out with the statement, "I am sorry that the accident occurred but I have accomplished what I aimed at. I have constructed a machine which can fly."

Hubert Latham (1883-1912) unsuccessfully attempts to fly the channel in Levavasseur's airleroned Antionette IV on July 19, 1909. Half French, half English, this skilful and popular aviator always flew Antoinettes, arguably the finest of the early monoplanes.

Blériot type XI, a similar model to the plane in which Blériot was first to fly the English channel on July 25, 1909, in the outstanding aeronautical event of the year. It was a somewhat perilous flight - Charles Dollfus remarked "no pilot of today, no matter how great, could repeat this exploit in such an aircraft and with such an engine".

BLÉRIOT'S CROSS-CHANNEL FLIGHT
Flight, 1909

Blériot's great success is a fitting sequel to Latham's splendid failure; there should be no jealousy in comparison, both are working in the cause of flight. M. Blériot reflects glory on his defeated rival at the same time that he is crowned with the laurels of victory himself. And M. Blériot deserves his success; how much, none save those who have followed his history in flight know. There were days not long since when M. Blériot used to tumble with his machine with almost monotonous persistency; yet he kept on, in spite of criticisms. In those days, too, he was still trying to fly a monoplane, and monoplanes were not very popular just then, for there were not wanting critics who almost went as far as saying that they would not fly at all. M. Blériot is the champion of the monoplane, and he has done more than anyone else to develop it. Moreover, he is engineer and pilot combined and the machine with which he has crossed the Channel, and thereby traced his name indelibly on the pages of history, is his own machine, the work of his own brain, and if the truth were known, contains, we dare say, a good deal of his own handicraft as well. He is not only a worker, he is a sportsman, is M. Blériot, and most thoroughly deserves every prize he has won.

It is rather apt to be forgotten how very early M. Blériot commenced his aviation experiences. As long ago as 1906 an illustration appeared in the Auto-motor Journal of May 26th, of an aeroplane which M. Blériot and Voisin had constructed for experimental work on Lake Enghien. It was a curious machine that, but it has this much of especial interest that it was designed for use over water. In the following year, 1907 M. Blériot had built and was trying at Issy, near Paris, a monoplane which does not differ in essentials from the machine which is on view this week at Selfridge's. What mishaps he used to have in those days! Almost every other time that he succeeded in getting off the ground he returned to earth with a crash; he always broke something, but it was never himself, always did this persevering pilot seem to bear a charmed life. As a matter of fact, he used to take

what precautions he could and he himself, as we mentioned last week, attributes many of his escapes to a little trick which he had of throwing himself on to one of the wings of his flyer when he saw that a catastrophe was imminent.

When M Blériot had advanced in the art of flight until he was easily among the two or three genuine pilots of the day, he conceived the idea of making quite a small machine, which type has since been known as his short-span flyer "No. 11." It was shown first of all at the Paris Salon at the end of last year, and attracted a very great deal of attention on account of its compact appearance. It was such a flyer as many had set their hearts upon, but as many more had deemed highly impractical.

No one foresaw then that this was to be the epoch making machine with which he should fly 25 miles across country on July 17th and 31 miles across the sea on July 25th. True, the dimensions of the span are somewhat larger as the result of alterations which followed various preliminary experiments, but that it is still to all intents and purposes the same compact machine must have been apparent to all who took the unique opportunity of seeing it at Dover or during the past few days in London at the Selfridge showrooms.

By his two great flights across country and across the Channel M. Blériot has set the seal of success upon the monoplane principle – his achievements are another huge step in the "coming of the monoplane." The monoplane is still by way of being the racer of the air. M. Blériot took roughly 40 minutes to cross the Channel, his speed being in the region of 45 miles an hour average, and according to his own account was nearer 50 miles an hour shortly after the start. That is a speed which only a limited number of pilots can be expected to feel safe at in their early experiments. Safety lies in speed, there is much reason to believe, but that is a different kind of safety, and is hardly in the reckoning if the pilot himself is not at home in the air under such conditions.

Blériot is now a master of the upper element, but he worked hard for his degree; on no occasion has his knowledge and skill stood him in better stead than during his Channel flight, for

Blériot on the occasion of his historic crossing of the channel. An engineer who came into aviation from the profitable business of manu-facturing automo-bile lamps, the Frenchman was later able to give up flying and set up a factory with a comfortably full order book for over 100 machines. By the start of World War I his company had constructed over 800 aero-planes of 40 different types.

The propeller blade, broken on landing, of the flimsy Blériot XI monoplane, powered by a 25 hp Anzani engine. The epic flight was accomplished without a compass.

there he met with difficulties which must surely have brought a less experienced and skillful pilot to sad grief.

Even at the start there was, according to M. Blériot's own estimate, a 10 knot wind; while, off Dover, the breeze was double this velocity, and the cliff currents particularly strong. In mid-Channel the wind had dropped, but at the moment of landing it was blowing in all directions.

The Story of the Flight

It was almost without warning, but nevertheless with a send off on the French shore from an enthusiastic crowd, M. Blériot flew across the Straits of Dover from Les Baraques, near Calais, to Northfall Meadow at Dover on Sunday July 25th thereby incidentally winning the Daily Mail £1,000 prize. Taking the weekend as a whole, it has been one of the windiest periods of a particularly unsettled summer and the previous day had in particular seemed hopeless for any cross-Channel flight. Half a gale had indeed been blowing, and a heavy sea running only a few hours before, and hence it is hardly to be wondered at that the feat was as totally unexpected as it was.

When this greatest of all great events in the annals of modern history was taking place the world and his wife were mostly abed, especially this side of the Channel. But M. Blériot had got up at half-past two in the morning, not feeling very well, had taken a short motor run just to blow the cob-webs away, and that was why he was able to snatch the one brief fine moment that presented itself between the daytime storms of Saturday and Sunday. Seeing that the fates were propitious, he then lost little time in bringing out the flyer, and in spite of his injured foot he quickly carried out a practice flight – over the sand–hills between Les Baraques and Sangatte. A little earlier, too, he had notified his intention to start to the destroyer "Escopette," which was consequently at that time standing out to sea, with Madame Blériot and others already aboard – all anxiously on the look out for him. Finding everything working properly with his machine, he speedily effected a fresh start, this time flying straight away over the cliffs and heading towards England.

That was at about twenty minutes to five (French time) and it was about twenty minutes past five (also French time) that he landed at Dover. Accounts differ as to the exact moment of departure and descent, and as a matter of fact

it is doubtful if any reliable timing was made since M. Blériot started without a watch as well as without a compass. The distance of the flight was about 31 miles, and hence the speed was in the region of 45 miles an hour. During the crossing he flew at an altitude of 150 ft. to 300 ft., and thus kept much nearer the water than Latham did on his attempt.

Blériot's monoplane quickly outstripped the torpedo-boat destroyer "Escopette," with which the French Government replaced the "Harpon," that was on duty during Latham's attempt in mid-Channel. M. Blériot lost sight of land and of his escort for a very uncomfortably long period – estimated by him to have been ten minutes – and was entirely without means of ascertaining his proper direction. In the circumstances he did the only thing possible, which was to keep straight on, and fortune favouring him, he sighted the English shore off Deal while heading for St. Margaret's Bay. Turning along the coast M. Blériot flew towards Dover, and put in at a gap in the cliffs where a representative of Le Martin, M. Fontaine, was signalling to him with a tricolour flag. The site on which the landing was accomplished was the Northfall Meadow. Although the arrival was noticed from afar by several, and M. Fontaine was on the chosen part of the cliff at Dover, yet even he failed to see the real landing, and P.C. Stanford was the only eye-witness of this great historic event, the landing on British soil of the first flyer to cross the Channel.

The actual contact with terra-firma was rather abrupt; in fact, not only was the propeller broken, but that part of the framework which carries the engine was also damaged. Mishaps of this sort, however, are absolutely negligible by comparison with the success of the main issue. Blériot had crossed the Channel, had won the Daily Mail prize and was none the worse for it, nor in all probability would his machine have been damaged had he been familiar with the site on which he was forced to alight.

One of the most interesting minor points associated with M. Blériot's cross-Channel flight is the manner in which at Dover he was heard afar off by the very few people who happened to be about at the time. The whirring of the motor (doubtless chiefly due to the open exhaust) was quite distinctly audible, according to more than one eye-witness, even while the flyer itself was a mere speck in the distance. The night watchman on the Promenade Pier, in relating his account of the proceedings to the Daily Telegraph, says: "I suddenly saw a peculiar object away to the eastward, moving very rapidly across the sky. As it came closer I could hear the whirring of the motor, and I judged that it was one of the flying men who had made a start and had practically got across." The chief officer of the Coastguard Station similarly relates that he could hear buzzing when the machine was several miles off.

Louis Blériot (1872-1936) testing at the first great aviation meeting at Reims in 1909, attended by such notables as Lloyd George, then Chancellor of the Exchequer, Lord Northcliffe and General French. "La Grande Semaine d'Aviation de la Champagne", under the patronage of the President of the Republic, was promoted and financed by the Champagne industry. An unqualified success, it was to set the fashion for many future meetings of the kind in Europe and the U.S.

Adolphe Pégoud at Brooklands in 1933. The first true exponent of aerobatics, or "stunts", including looping the loop, Pégoud, the "up-side down aviator", gave a most scientific exhibition - its value was soon to be proved in exchanges between Allied and Geman aeroplanes in France.

Wealthy English pioneer Claude Grahame-White ("I may say at once", he commented, "it costs rather more money to fly than a great many people believe".) became a national hero with his gallant but unsuccessful attempt to overtake Frenchman Louis Paulman in a race to fly from London to Manchester in 1910.

Barra (Maurice Farman), 3 hrs. 56 mins.; Renaux (Maurice Farman), 4 hrs. 8 mins. Men of the Nieuport factory gave Weymann a remarkable reception at the Gare de l'Est on his reaching Paris in the evening of the flight. This was not surprising seeing that he had won for the manufacturing firm the enormous prize of £32,000, offered by the French Government.

> The cavalry, in particular, were not friendly to the aeroplane, which it was believed, would frighten the horses.
>
> SIR WALTER RALEIGH
> *(writing of 1910)*

FROM THE CAR
Aeronautics
Weymann's Great Success at Reims

FROM FLIGHT
1911

Of all the events that have taken place during the military competitions at Reims, the most interesting has undoubtedly been the cross-country flight to Amiens and back, which took place on Monday of last week.

Many fliers of world-wide fame competed, and the best times taken over the 300 kilometres were as follows:- Weymann (Nieuport machine), 2 hrs. 34 mins.; Prevost (Deperdussin), 3 hrs. 21 mins.; Fischer (Henry Farman), 3 hrs. 33 mins.;

A few years ago crowds used to assemble to see a motor car, and the generation that produced the automobile is now assembled in honour of the aeroplane.

Brooklands itself was built for the car, yet it is the aeroplane that attracts most people to its grounds. How soon and to what extent will the aeroplane invade the territory of the car as a useful and everyday sort of vehicle must have been a question in the minds of many of those who looked on at the start of the Circuit of Britain on Saturday.

It became fashionable for ladies to make at least one flight with a "flying man". Grahame White, who auctioned passenger flights in his Farman, is pictured here assisting a female. Constantly in the news, he was the first to fly at night.

FROM THE DAILY MIRROR
1911

The vastness of the crowd was the strongest possible testimony of the magnitude of the interest taken in this world test of airmanship.

It was an enthusiastic, joyous, picnic crowd which probably numbered 50,000 people. Nearly every motor car, with hood drawn over to keep off the glare of the sun (it was 90°F in the shade), had its picnic party.

Besides being vast and enthusiastic, it was a crowd representative of every country in Europe and the United States. Well known men from France, Germany, Italy and America, assembled here for the purpose of noting the various types of machines taking part in the most practical flying race ever organised.

Among these deeply interested visitors were the Kaiser's brother, Prince Henry of Prussia, and General von Nieber, chief of the German flying staff.

The Prince was very much concerned when Lieut. Porte, of the British Navy, had a nasty accident.

Lieut. Porte was the third airman to start. His machine, a Deperdussin Monoplane, rose from the ground after some delay caused by a leak, and in making a turn at an acute climbing angle, crashed to the ground on the left wing, throwing up an enormous cloud of dust.

There was a painful silence, which was soon broken by cheers when the young officer was seen to walk, evidently unharmed, from under the wreckage.

FROM THE DAILY MIRROR
1911

Following André Beaumont of France came Astley – the sort of young English man whom one would expect to be an airman – and then Compton Paterson on the "Baby" Grahame-White biplane who provided the sensation of the afternoon.

He arrived, circled the ground, turned round and skimmed the grass directly towards the crowd of people. It looked as though he couldn't stop – as if the machine had got out of control.

An accident seemed inevitable. But he skirted the far end of the southern enclosure and turned round into the narrow lane in front of the hangars or sheds.

Then it dawned on the crowd that he was really flying to his shed – flying right into his stable. A great cheer broke out and a chauffeur, gasping with enthusiasm shouted: "It's easier than turning into Bond Street!"

Last of all came Lieut. Bier, the Austrian representative, and at eight o'clock he was to be seen high up against the gorgeous red clouds of the sunset. It was a fitting finish. There were the clouds and the air and the sky, unaltered since the dawn of man, and high up amongst them

34

this new phenomenon – the aeroplane – serenely representing man's latest challenge and conquest.

From The Field
1911

Londoners seem scarcely aware of the splendid exhibition of flying that can be seen any fine day at Brooklands. They appear also to imagine that if the weather be dull or foggy in town it is the same every where else. By the way, it might be well for the Brooklands authorities to arrange to have displayed in some conspicuous position at Waterloo Station, and somewhere in the West End also, daily statements as to the weather at Weybridge. Often when it is dull in London it is sunny and warm there although such a little way out from town.

Saturdays are the busiest flying days, of course, but Brooklands is well worth visiting on other days in the week. There are about 50 machines in the aerodrome. Some of the aviators are quite brilliant flyers and the Brooklands centre has peculiar interest on account of the variety of types of aeroplane at work, Frenchmen, Englishmen, and ladies, can be seen flying and learning to fly, and passenger flights are common. Flights can be booked beforehand in London if desired.

A typical Edwardian flying display. The thrill of seeing fragile creations guided precariously through the air was the draw, and large crowds assembled for such demonstrations. Bristol's flying school at Brooklands, under the direction of Captain H.F, Wood used boxkites for primary training,and a French design, the Prier, for more advanced tuition.

A Bristol boxkite. A contemporary report of this reads: "Sir George White ordered another flight, midst ringing cheers. M. Tedard, the famous French aviator, took his seat on the biplane and circled the downs . . . he landed lightly as a bird in a space kept clear by the police".

FROM THE CAR
1912

M. Eugene Renaux, was promoted by the French Government on New Year's Day to be a Chevalier of the Legion of Honour. His military aviation work is thus officially rewarded. The British New Year's honours list, on the other hand, contained no recognition of anybody's services to aeronautical science or practical aviation.

Much regret will be felt at the death of Reichelt, the inventor of a parachute intended to save aviators from destruction. The parachute was constructed as a special kind of clothing. Having been allowed by the authorities to test the apparatus at the Eiffel Tower on Saturday morning, Reichelt jumped from the first platform of the Tower and was killed immediately.

We do not consider that aeroplanes will be of any possible use for war purposes.

THE BRITISH SECRETARY OF STATE FOR WAR
(1910)

A machine is the embodiment of human thought, and if it sometimes seems to be almost alive, that is because it springs of live parents.

SIR WALTER RALEIGH

Keep the aeroplane in such an attitude that the air pressure is always directly in the pilot's face.

BARBER (1916)

I hate to shoot a Hun down without him seeing me, for although this method is in accordance with my doctrine, it is against what little sporting instincts I have left.

B. MCCUDDEN, V.C. (1917)

A Zurich flying poster from 1910. The first flights from Switzerland were made by the German Captain Engelhardt on his Wright A. from the ice-covered lake at St. Moritz on March 13, 1910.

When my brother and I built and flew the first man-carrying flying machine, we thought that we were introducing into the world an invention which would make further wars practically impossible.

ORVILLE WRIGHT (1917)

Upon the whole, the writer is glad to believe that when man succeeds in flying through the air the ultimate effect will be to diminish greatly the frequency of wars and to substitute some more rational methods of settling international misunderstandings. This may come to pass not only because of the additional horrors which will result in battle, but because no part of the field will be safe, no matter how distant from the actual scene of conflict. . . . A chance explosive dropped from a flying machine may destroy the chiefs, disorganize the plans, and bring confusion to the stronger or more skilfully led side.

So, may it be; let us hope that the advent of a successful flying machine, now only dimly foreseen and nevertheless thought to be possible, will bring nothing but good into the world; that it shall abridge distance, make all parts of the globe accessible, bring men into closer relation with each other, advance civilisation, and hasten the promised era in which there shall be nothing but peace and good will among all men.

OCTAVE CHANUTE (1894)

MUCH FASTER
The Car, 1912

In a strong north-west wind, Gilmour made an excellent flight on Wednesday from Hendon to Brooklands on the Martin-Handasyde mono-plane. Not knowing the country, being without map or compass, and fearing that he would be blown to the south-east and over Ealing and Brentford, he held over too far to the west, and found himself practically at Slough, only discovering his mistake by seeing Staines reservoirs away on his left. Turning then to the south, he reached Brooklands in just twenty minutes from leaving Hendon, having covered at least 23 miles as measured over the ground, and rather more in the air, allowing for the fact that he was fighting his way into the wind most of the time. The machine must be much faster than the 65 miles an hour with which it is credited.

This morning at 3:15, Wilbur passed away, aged 45 years, 1 month and 14 days. A short life full of consequences, an unfailing intellect, imperturbable temper, great self-reliance and as great modesty, seeing the right clearly, pursuing it steadily, he lived and died.

BISHOP MILTON WRIGHT
(in his diary, dated May 30th 1912)

The legendary Sopwith Camel appeared in 1916, at first fitted with a 130 hp Clerget and later the 200 hp Bentley B.R.2. rotary engine. The Camel - its name came from the hump on the engine cowling which housed two machine-guns - made an invaluable contribution to the Allied war effort.

THE RED BARON
1917

"One of the English aeroplanes, a Sopwith one-seater, attacked us and we saw immediately that the enemy aeroplane was superior to ours. Only because we were three against one we detected the enemy's weak point. I managed to get behind him and shot him down."

ACES OF THE AIR
By Royston Capel

Towards the end of what had been a glorious summer in 1914 the first, possibly the truest, Golden Age of flying drew to a close, giving way to a steelier, more ominous horizon.

War was declared, but since it was all going to be over by Christmas, "the many" were unconcerned by the infant service formed by the chief protagonists in the immediate preceding years.

The prescient few, however, such as Tommy Sopwith, Anton Fokker and Igor Sikorsky foresaw a much longer confrontation, with aircraft assuming increasingly wide and diverse roles in the conflict that would require more than the "winged bathchairs" of the present generation.

By mid 1915 the opposing armies had become bogged down in a static war and recon-

naissance became a vital adjunct to military intelligence. Fighter aircraft, designated "scouts", were rapidly developed to counter this new threat, and speed, manoeuvrability, climb-rate and fire-power soon became the vital qualities of these craft. The problems involved in satisfying these separate requirements were solved in varying degrees, at various times, by the main combatants – the British, French and Germans. The latter, with their well-developed expertise in small arms, were the first to perfect the fixed, forward firing, synchronous machine gun. The French, by quaint contrast, solved the same problem by fitting metal deflector blades to the back of the propeller – surprisingly, the system was quite effective.

The scene was now set for the emergence of the "Fighter Aces" and the world's press, starved of action and successes on the Western Front, picked up the idea, invented by the French, to denote a pilot who had notched up five victories. Curiously, while the Americans adopted this on their entry to the War in 1917, the British and the Germans never did. The former decided it was unfair to single out the successful few and neglect the many whose contribution was equally important. The German method was to reward their pilots with certain decorations for a certain number of victories. The epithet used was Oberkanone – almost, "Top Gun".

Finally, before describing the "Aces" and their tallies of victories it is worth remembering that

during World War I the lack of camera guns and radio communications meant that victories were much harder to confirm than they are today. As a result, many of the pilots had a far greater number of "kills" than those with which they were officially credited.

The Red Baron

The highest scoring ace of World War I was Rittmeister (Cavalry Captain) Manfred Freiherr von Richthofen – the "Red Baron". Born on May 2, 1892, he was credited with 80 victories; he was a hero to Germany, and grudgingly admired even by his enemies.

Richtofen started his war service as a cavalryman on the Eastern Front and transferred to the flying service in May 1915. Until late 1916, he flew reconnaissance aircraft without much distinction, but was then moved, quite fortuitously, to a scout squadron on the Western Front. Within days he had achieved his first victory; by January 1917 he had won the "Blue Max", the *Order Pour Le Mérite*. He brought a cold – almost ruthless – quality to aerial combat, commissioning a silver cup that bore the details of each of his victims. In April, 1917, Richthofen shot down 21 aircraft – no doubt to his silversmith's delight.

Rittmeister ("Cavalry Captain") Count Manfred von Richthofen, credited with 80 victories, was found dead in the cockpit of his triplane with a bullet wound to the chest, 21 days after the Royal Flying Corps and the Royal Naval Air Service had merged to form the Royal Air Force.

Inset Left:
A Farman "Shorthorn", which earned the sobriquet "Horace", employed a 60 hp Gnome engine producing a speed of 62 mph. The Royal Navy Air Service used these planes extensively at the start of the World War I.

The R.E.8, introduced in 1916. Distinctive vertical exhausts, a large airscoop and air-cooled engine were characteristics of this fighter-reconnaisance type, not the quickest of aeroplanes.

A Nieuport fighter of 1917. The earliest Nieuport was derived from the Blériot monoplane. At first, armaments were carried experimentally in aircraft, and the 1911 Nieuport, with its machine gun, was one of the first machines to be designed or adapted for warlike use.

The Red Baron's ruthlessness, possibly the result of his aristocratic background, extended to enemy flyers and civilians alike. At one airfield in Belgium, he threatened to have villagers summarily shot unless they immediately dug the bogged-down planes in his squadron out of the mud in which they had stuck.

After nine months on the Western Front, Richthofen was given command of four Jastas, or squadrons, that became known as "Richthofen's Flying Circus", from the bright, almost garish colours used by pilots to identify their machines.

On April 21, 1918, the Red Baron was chasing an inexperienced allied pilot at low level. Captain Ray Brown, flying a Sopwith Camel, happened on the chase and let fly a burst at long range. Richtofen's Fokker D1 Triplane broke away and made a forced landing without apparent damage. But Richtofen was found dead – with a bullet in his chest.

The great tactician

The first great fighter pilot tactician was a German pilot called Hauptmann Oswald Boelcke. Born on May 9, 1891 he began operational flying in September 1914, and by mid

1915 was piloting an armed aircraft (as opposed to an unarmed reconnaissance plane). He quickly realized that instead of operating as individuals the scouts (as fighter planes were first named) should fly together in squadrons and take the action to the enemy. Boelcke augmented this simple idea by developing training programmes for his pilots, teaching both individual skills and squadron tactics. Soon, he was given command of Jagdstaffel 2, equipped with Albatross D1 and D2 aircraft, which became the first crack air unit of the Western Front. Many of the great German fighter pilots served their apprenticeships with this unit.

On October 28, 1916, Boelcke banked steeply during a dog-fight. His wing struck the undercarriage of one of his own planes, and Boelcke spiralled quickly to the ground. At the age of 25, he had 40 victories.

The Eagle of Lille

One of Germany's first fighter aces was Lieutenant Max Immelman, "The Eagle of Lille". In mid 1915, Immelman's unit was equipped with the new Fokker E1 monoplane scout. Its great manoeuvrability and forward-firing synchronized gun quickly earned it the soubriquet "The

The world's first properly stable aeroplane the De Havilland B.E.2c designed at the Royal Aircraft factory and used for reconnaissance. Equipped at first with a revolver or rifle and later a sideways-firing machine gun. "The early war pilot went into battle armed more as a sportsman than as a soldier" remarked one R.F.C. officer.

Fokker Scourge" in the part of the Front around Douai. Immelman was a fine pilot, best remembered for inventing the "Immelman Turn", a great manoeuvre that enabled a pilot to outturn a pursuer and get on to his tail. But this technique was of little use on June 18, 1916, when Immelman attacked an FE2b over Lens. During the attack, a second FE2b fired on him, and Immelman went into a steep dive; the aircraft broke up in mid-air. At the time, his tally was 15 victories.

Charging the enemy

The first of the British aces was Captain Albert Ball VC. This was partly on account of his technical skill, partly due to his habit of charging straight at the enemy, regardless of their number. At any rate, Ball accounted for 47 German aircraft.

Ball's favourite plane was a French Nieuport scout, which lacked the sophisticated synchronized machine gun of his opponents. Imagine attacking an enemy formation of six or seven aircraft head-on at full speed while aiming and firing a Lewis gun mounted on a large swivel ring on the upper wing with one hand, the other hand to control the plane! Nonetheless, Ball was inordinately successful, and was lionised by the British public.

After a spell in England instructing new pilots, Ball returned to France with an extraordinary roving commission, that allowed him to hunt the enemy on his own – the other members of his squadron probably heaved a sigh of relief. On May 6, 1917, though, Ball dived into cloud to follow a German single - seater plane. It never emerged, and his wrecked plane was later found near Lens. Ball's body was unmarked, and his death remains a mystery; he was not yet 21.

Implacable Mannock

The highest scoring of all British pilots was Major Edward "Mick" Mannock VC. Officially with 73 victories to his credit, Mannock is known to have insisted that several of his own kills were attributed to young pilots serving under his command.

Born on May 24, 1887, Mannock was already a comparatively old man by the time he qualified as a pilot in November 1916; in fact, it is remarkable that he was ever accepted for flying duty in the first place, since he suffered from astigmatism in the left eye. Like Ball, he started

Factory Workers at Short Bros in 1919. Eustace and Oswald Short had developed a prosperous business manufacturing balloons for the richer amateur aeronauts of the time, such as the Hon. Chas Rolls and Moore-Brabazon before turning full time to building aeroplanes.

The De Havilland DH4, the most effective of the specialised light bombers. Faster, and with a better rate of climb than many German fighters, some 5,000 were built in America.

42

his combat career in a Nieuport scout , and later transferred to an SE5a. But unlike Ball, or any other Allied ace, Mannock was a bitter, implacable fighter, showing no mercy whatever to the enemy, men or machines.

Apart from his individual skill, Mannock is remembered as an innovative patrol leader – probably the greatest of all in the Allies. He instituted the principle of meticulous planning and briefing before each and every sortie, with the result that no patrol he led was ever "bounced" by the enemy.

On July 26, 1918, Mannock's SE5a was hit in the fuel tank by a stray bullet from the German trenches, and neither his aircraft nor his body was ever found. He had fallen victim to fire – the greatest fear of British pilots, since, unlike all other nations, the British High Command doggedly refused to allow parachutes in the aircraft on the grounds that to do so might encourage defeatism.

A natural pilot

The most successful of the British Empire pilots was Canadian Major William Avery Bishop VC, with 72 victories.

Born in Ontario on February 8, 1894, Bishop came to Britain with the Canadian Mounted Rifles as a cavalry subaltern in 1915, before transferring to the Royal Flying Corps. At first, he flew as an observer, but was hospitalized with frostbite – a reminder that flying at 90mph at 12,000ft in an air temperature of between 0° and -20°C carries other risks than enemy action or ground fire.

Bishop subsequently became a pilot and joined 60 Squadron in March 1917, flying a French Nieuport 17 scout. A natural pilot, Bishop's scoring rate was nothing short of phenomenal. During his first two months of combat, flying for seven hours a day, he downed 20 enemy aircraft; on one day he attacked 19 aircraft in nine separate engagements, shooting down two of them.

By early 1918, as one of the few British aces still alive, Bishop was taken off combat duty and devoted his time to recruiting and gunnery instruction. But by late May, 1918, he had managed to persuade the authorities to let him return to France – on the strict understanding that he kept well clear of trouble. Within 12 days, Bishop had shot down another 25 aircraft and was recalled to Britain, never to fly operationally again. He remained in the Service and died in 1956, with the prestigious rank of Honorary Air Marshal.

Black Maria

Britain's Royal Naval Air Service also had a distinguished Canadian ace in its ranks: Captain Raymond Collishaw. With 60 victories, occupying third place in the table of British and Empire aces, he was the only one of the top five not to be awarded a VC.

Born in British Columbia on November 22,

Inset Left:
**Short Bros,
Rochester, Kent in
1919. Shorts' work
was mainly for the
Navy, and in 1912
Horace acquired a
new factory at
Rochester on the
River Medway with
brother Oswald in
charge of produc-
tion. A modest
number of staff -
some twelve
workers
was originally
employed.**

Top Right:
**The war proved to
an enormous
stimulus to the
progress of scien-
tific and technical
development. Here
is the principle
French fighter the
S.P.A.D. (1916)
attacking a balloon.
The S.P.A.D. was
flown by American,
British, Russian,
Italian and Belgium
pilots, as well as
Frenchmen.**

**S. Pania's humor-
ous cartoon,
portraying his
impressions of
enthusiasm for the
flying machine and
the motor car,
speaks for itself.**

1893, Collishaw served in the merchant marine,
transferring to the RNAS at the beginning of
1916. He was operational by August, flying a
Sopwith 1½-strutter – in fact, he spent the
whole of his operational career flying Sopwiths.

In December 1916 he was shot down, but
survived unhurt, and in April 1917, flying a
Sopwith Pup, he was transferred to No 10
Squadron to command the legendary "B" flight
of Sopwith triplanes. Its aircraft were painted
black – Collishaw's personal machine being
named "Black Maria", the others being called
"Black Prince", "Black Roger", "Black Sheep"
and "Black Death". This unit, flown entirely by
Canadians, earned a fearsome reputation: between May and July, 87 enemy aircraft were shot

The 360 hp, ABC-engined Sopwith Dragon. With the coming of peace T. O. M. Sopwith started a new company named after his friend and chief test pilot, the brilliant Harry Hawker. Under the design leadership of the great Sydney Camm, and with Sopwith himself as chairman, the Hawker Aircraft Company brought the biplane to its peak of perfection between 1928 and 1939.

down, Collishaw accounting for 16 of them in 27 days (including three on a single day).

At the end of July, with his score at 38, Collishaw was shot down again but once more survived unhurt. In November he transferred to a Sopwith Camel, to see out the remainder of the War – but he stayed in the Royal Air Force to serve with distinction in World War II, with the rank of Air Vice Marshal.

The lone hunter

The fourth highest scoring British and Empire ace was Major James Thomas Byford McCudden VC, with 57 victories. Having joined the Royal Engineers as a bugler in 1910, he transferred to the Royal Flying Corps in 1913, arriving in France as a mechanic in August 1914. By June 1915, he was a sergeant, making unofficial flights as an observer and student pilot; by December 1915 he was in combat as an observer, and in January of the next year he was posted home as flight sergeant to be trained as a pilot. In August, back in France, he joined a fighter squadron equipped with DH2s.

As a skilful pilot with an unrivalled knowledge of the mechanics of both aircraft and armaments, McCudden was famed for stalking his victims over long distances, using every available scrap of cloud cover. While recognized as being an excellent patrol leader, he very much preferred to act as a lone hunter – on more than one occasion shooting down four planes in a single day.

But on February 25, 1918, McCudden shot

victories. Born in the Vosges in 1894, he was a keen aviation buff before the War – in the way of these things, therefore, he was mobilized in 1914 into an engineer battalion, where he spent his days digging trenches. In February 1915, though, he started flying training, and joined an unarmed reconnaissance squadron in June 1915.

A courageous and resourceful pilot, Fonck spent a year in this squadron, frequently nursing seriously damaged planes back to his base. In July 1916 he fitted a machine gun to his aircraft and within a few weeks he had forced down an enemy Rumpler, whose crew surrendered. His second victory came in March 1917, and now a recognized fighter pilot, Fonck's career burgeoned. On a number of occasions during 1917 he shot down two planes on one day, but in May 1918 he downed six planes in a single day – and he repeated this feat in September. Bearing in mind the limited amount of ammunition that these diminutive planes could carry, this bears testimony to Fonck's extraordinary skill and economy with his gunnery – sometimes he used as few as five or six rounds to shoot down an aircraft. A remarkable master of the art of deflection shooting, and arguably the most successful World War I fighter pilot of all, Fonck died peacefully in his Paris home in 1953.

The frail ace

The second most successful French ace was Capitaine Georges Marie Ludovic Jules Guynemer, with 54 victories. Born on December 24, 1894, Guynemer was so frail that he was twice rejected for military service. But having been accepted as a trainee mechanic in November 1914, he was able to train and qualify as a pilot in June 1915.

Within a year, Guynemer had eight victories to his credit, and soon his tally began to rise quickly. But what really endeared him to the French public was fragile health and physical frailty, combined with the fact that he had been shot down seven times. When he was shot down and killed by Lieutenant Wisseman in September 1917, the nation mourned. Wisseman, though, was himself killed by René Fonck some three weeks later.

down his last aircraft and was recalled – like many other aces at the time – to Britain to recruit and train others. He was awarded the Victoria Cross, Britain's highest decoration, in April, and, as Major McCudden, was posted to command 60 Squadron. Shortly afterwards, taking-off to join his new command, his engine failed, and, amazingly, McCudden committed the most basic of pilot errors: he tried to turn back to the airfield. With low flying speed and no height, this manoeuvre was almost invariably fatal. There was no exception in McCudden's case.

The master gunner

The most successful of all Allied aces was Frenchman Capitaine Réné Paul Fonck, with 75

The racing driver

America's most successful ace was Captain Edward Vernon Rickenbacker, who had 26 victories to his name.

Born on October 8, 1890, in Columbus, Ohio, he had an extremely successful career as a racing driver before World War I, and became interested in flying while on a visit to Britain in early 1917. On America's entry into the War, in April 1917, he proposed the formation of a racing drivers' squadron. The idea was received with enthusiasm, though Rickenbacker was posted to an "Aviation Instruction Centre" as an engineering officer.

Nevertheless, Rickenbacker took flying lessons privately, and following pilot qualification, he joined the 94th Aero Squadron in March 1918. It took him six weeks to achieve his first victory, but by the end of May Rickenbacker had qualified as an ace. An ear infection grounded him until September, but by the Armistice that ended the War in November he had destroyed a further 21 enemy aircraft.

But this did not mark the end of Rickenbacker's remarkable career. Between the Wars, he was responsible for building up Eastern Airlines, and then he flew operationally again during World War II. He was forced to ditch during the Pacific Campaign and he and his crew survived for 21 days on a life raft. Rickenbacker died at the age of 82, in August 1973.

The maverick balloon buster

America's second greatest ace, with 21 victories was an all-American, anti-authoritarian maverick called Lieutenant Frank Luke Jr. Born in Phoenix, Arizona, on May 19, 1897, Luke was a fine athlete and an excellent shot. His youth was rough and tough, spent around Arizona's copper mines, where he acquired a reputation as a man not to be crossed.

When America entered the War, Luke enlisted in a signals squadron, gaining a commission in January 1918. After several brushes with authority, he transferred to 27th Aero Squadron in July, where he was regarded as cocky and truculent even by his colleagues – no shrinking violets themselves. However, his considerable flying skill and outstanding marksmanship, combined with embittered aggression, made him a great combat pilot.

"Balloon busting" became Luke's speciality, and he forged a remarkable partnership with his wingman – and only close friend – Lieutenant Wehner. The Germans used balloons extensively as artillery observation platforms, and they were always very well protected indeed, with fighters flying top cover, anti-aircraft batteries and concentrated small arms flying below. Luke and Wehner seemed to regard this as a personal challenge.

The Luke-Wehner partnership began on Sep-

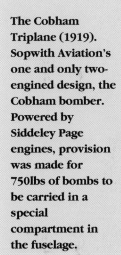

tember 14, and by September 18 it had downed 11 balloons and five aircraft. On that day, though, Luke returned to his base elated, only to find that Wehner had been killed. On September 26, he lost his replacement wingman, Lieutenant Roberts, and went absent for a day, deeply depressed.

The next day, Luke took off on an unauthorized flight and shot down another balloon, spending the night at a French airfield. By now he was in utter disgrace, and orders grounding him had been issued. Luke's response was to refuel at a forward airfield, then fly over his Headquarters, dropping a note that read: "Watch three Hun balloons on the Meuse Lake".

He shot down the first balloon, but was badly wounded while shooting down the second; nevertheless, Luke flew on and disposed of the third. He then strafed German troops in Murvaux, eventually crash-landing in the outskirts of the village. When called on to surrender, he opened fire with his revolver, only to fall back, riddled with bullets – just like one of his Wild West forbears. It was not until after the War that his grave was located and the story pieced together from eye-witness accounts.

The Cobham Triplane (1919). Sopwith Aviation's one and only two-engined design, the Cobham bomber. Powered by Siddeley Page engines, provision was made for 750lbs of bombs to be carried in a special compartment in the fuselage.

The final tally

As a postscript to this account of some of the great fighter aces of World War I, the number of pilots in each of the combatant air forces that achieved the coveted five victories or more is given below:

British and British Empire ?	784
German	363
French	158
American	88
Italian	43
Austro-Hungarian	28
Russian	19
Belgian	5

His (Capt. Maitland's) life, though it ended in its prime, was surprisingly long, for he had made danger his friend, and in the advancement of the cause to which he dedicated himself had welcomed every risk.

The air service still flourishes; its health depends on a secret elixir of immortality, which enables a body to repair its severest losses. The name of this elixir is tradition, and the greatest of all the achievements of the air service is that in a very few years, under the hammer of war, it has fashioned and welded its tradition, and has made it sure. Critics who speak of what they have not felt and do not know have sometimes blamed the air service because, being young, it has not the decorum of age. The Latin poet said that it is decorous to die for one's country; in that decorum the service is perfectly instructed.

SIR WALTER RALEIGH

"HELLS ANGELS"
1930

"Hells Angels," now being presented at the London Pavilion, is a film which no one who has any interest in the air should miss. Its photography is marvellous and certainly by far the best which has ever been seen on the screen in connection with aircraft.

But – and a very large but – there is no doubt that Howard Hughes, its producer, will not gain the whole-hearted support of ex-R.F.C officers and men. It seems little short of incredible that one who has spent such colossal sums – the film is reputed to have cost $400,000 to produce – on obtaining real war-time aircraft and the services of a staff of flying experts and pilots, the size of which make the staff of an aerial transport company look small, should almost entirely neglect the accuracy of every detail of the film except the flying side. Though even here it was asking much to expect us to stomach tight Formation flying at night in search of Zeppelins.

On Tuesday night, one could hear snorts of derision all around from those who looked upon the farcical representation of R.F.C. officers, their uniform, their behaviour and, in fact, everything they said and did except flying, as a direct insult to the Service. But, and again a large "but," the misrepresentation of the facts did not stop at the depiction of the R.F.C., it extended into all the personal scenes not actually connected with flying. Why Hughes did not engage an English actress instead of a blatantly "American" one is understandable. Why, when spending so lavishly on

the production, he did not enlist the services of one of those Englishmen, whom we are told are numerous in Hollywood since the advent of the Talkies, to anglicise the internal decoration of the houses, the furniture, the doors of the rooms, the labels on the shop windows, the postal service and their method of delivering letters and, in fact, the whole non-flying side of the film, is quite beyond comprehension. Why try and make it in English at all if it is not going to be done properly? No doubt as it stands it will pass for English in America, but we are told that its consumption over here will be even more important.

The story itself is, of course, weak, and the general behaviour of those who are entrusted with catering for that section of the public who cannot do without their "Love Interest," very sloppy, but, unlike other flying films we have recently had thrust upon us from America, "Hell's Angels" triumphs over these faults – seemingly totally unnecessary faults – by virtue of its incredibly magnificent photography. The finest of the scenes are naturally centred round the Zeppelin – a real one, which we are told was built at a great cost by the Goodyear Zeppelin

Turn-of-the-century artist "Gamy" is thought to be Margeurite Montaut, wife of Ernest. Aeronautics, motor cycling and speed boats were preferred subjects, as well as the motor car.

"Gamy" here depicts Paulhan in the *Daily Mail* London to Manchester Race of 1910. These prints were probably hand-tinted by professional colourists working freehand using watercolour.

On January 1, 1914, Tony Jannus took off for Tampa, in Florida, from St. Petersburg, also in America, in a Benoist airboat. The journey of some 23 minutes marked the beginning of scheduled flying by the Airboat Line.

Pilots and demonstrators were encouraged to make more and more audacious flights to capture the attention of a public that was showing increasing interest in aviation. For this display, the ringmaster was C.W.A. Scott, aviation editor of *The News Chronicle*.

Corp. In describing the arrival of this airship through a cloud one would be in the greatest danger of detracting from its majestic beauty if one were to say more than that it is the greatest masterpiece of photography ever seen on the screen. The subsequent aerial combats – using S.E 5's, Camels, Avro's, Snipes, Fokker D.VII's and a Gotha – and the final destruction of the Zeppelin, are marvellous, especially this latter, though one cannot help but regret that its presentation should have come so close on the heels of the disaster to R 101. We imagine this fact will reflect greatly on the film's popularity.

Taken all round, "Hell's Angels" is a most magnificent film, which comes within an ace of being ruined – for this country at any rate – through lack of attention to details which should have been correctly presented. It appears that Hughes has been so bitten with the idea that he was going to produce an unsurpassable flying film that he considered the rest of the story unimportant, with the result that there is a far too well defined line between the excellence of the one and the inferiority of the other.

From the point of view of the cost of production a few details are interesting. The staff of

pilots was some 137 and the two chief actors had to learn to fly for the purposes of the film.

Not one of the aerial scenes is faked and all the crashes shown are real. Reports vary as to the number of pilots who were killed during the production, but it would appear to be between three and seven.

The film has taken since 1926 to produce, though the actual filming did not start until October, 1927. A complete aerodrome was maintained in California as the main base and a second representing the one from which Baron Von Richthofen operated during the war.

One of the Fokker D VII's used is reputed to be one of the actual machines used in Richthofen's "Circus," and during the production of "Hell's Angels" it flew over 400 hours.

One other point worthy of mention is the sound and dialogue. This is the best we have heard and in most cases the aeroplane engine noises come through quite realistically instead of being a blurred jumble of harsh sounds.

In view of the size of the production it did seem as if the film was somewhat short, especially as we have been told by people who actually took part all about the mass of material which had been cut out, but, as it is, the interest is sustained until the last moment.

An uninterrupted navigable ocean, that comes to the threshold of every man's door, ought not to be neglected as a source of human gratification and advantage.

SIR GEORGE CAYLEY (1816)

I have not the smallest molecule of faith in aerial navigation other than ballooning.

LORD KELVIN (1896)

AERIAL ADVENTURES

"The engine is the heart of an aeroplane, but the pilot is its soul"

Sir Walter Raleigh

First across the Atlantic - a postcard commemorating the first direct non-stop crossing of the Atlantic in a converted Vickers Vimy bomber. Pilot and navigator both received knighthoods from King George V.

Commercial air transport continued to progress, and seen here is the B.A.T., typical of the period and manufactured by the British Aerial Transport Company of Willesden.

VICKERS-VIMY-ROLLS.

The first direct flight across the Atlantic.
JUNE 14-15 1919.
Capt. Sir John Alcock K.B.E. D.S.C.-Pilot.
Lieut. Sir Arthur Whitten Brown K.B.E.-Navigator.

Before take-off, a professional pilot is keen, anxious, but lest someone read his true feelings, he is elaborately casual. The reason for this is that he is about to enter a new though familiar world. The process of entrance begins a short time before he leaves the ground and is completed the instant he is in the air. From that moment on, not only his body but his spirit and personality exist in a separate world known only to himself and his comrades.

As the years go by, he returns to this invisible world rather than to the earth for peace and solace. There he also finds a profound enchantment although he can seldom describe it. He can discuss it with others of his kind, and because they, too, know and feel its power they understand. But his attempts to communicate his feelings to his wife or other earthly confidants invariably end in failure. Flying is hypnotic and all pilots are willing victims to the spell. Their world is like a magic island in which the factors of life and death assume their proper values. Thinking becomes clear because there are no earthly foibles or embellishments to confuse it. Professional pilots are, of necessity uncomplicated, simple men. Their thinking must remain straightforward, or they die – violently.

E.K. Gann

FROM THE TIMES
1919

At the start visibility was very good, but the Newfoundland fog bank could be seen ahead, and we were soon flying between a bank of clouds and the fog. We did not see either the sea or sky for a period of seven hours with the exception of an occasional glimpse at both, in small patches.

As the light failed, worse conditions were encountered and clouds and fog became denser; eventually we were flying in the bank of fog. Suddenly we struck a clear patch in the bank of clouds where Brown was able to check his position from a sight of the Pole Star, Vega, and the moon. This lasted half-an-hour; however, later thick fog together with bad bumps impeded him from holding his course.

The machine then started to spin, caused through the airspeed indicator failing to register, probably due to the pilot tube which had been damaged when the wireless generator propeller was blown away. (The wireless generator propeller shaft sheared ten minutes after take off.)

The spin started at a height of 4,000 feet. We rapidly lost height, and on coming out of the mist found ourselves very close to the water at a dangerous angle. Upon seeing the horizon I was able to regain control and put the machine on its true course.

A Pan American flight schedule and baggage sticker that lists the West Indies and Central American destinations on the "Lindbergh Circle" route. The circular Caribbean routes were surveyed by Lindberg with the *Spirit of St. Louis* and a Sikorsky S-38 in 1929.

Climbing again to 7,000 feet through thick fog we saw the moon once or twice, but Brown was unable to obtain any readings. We continued to climb steadily, trying to get above the fog, and were still climbing at daybreak in large banks of cloud which we could not get above. This continued for about five or six hours; hail and sleet were encountered which caused the radiator shutters to become jammed, also obscuring our petrol sight gauge and choking up the pilot tube. We climbed steadily to 11,000 feet, hoping to get above the clouds and take further readings from the sun. At this height we saw the sun several times trying to force its way through the clouds and Brown eventually succeeded in fixing his position.

After this we decided to descend, and almost reached the surface of the sea before obtaining clear visibility. There the wind was blowing very strongly from the south-west. To counteract this Brown thought it advisable to steer a more south-easterly course. We had been flying in this direction for about forty minutes when we saw the two islands of Eeshal and Turk, but we could not see the mainland owing to rain and low clouds. The mainland was not visible until we were practically over it, and even then only the hills.

> This is earth again, the earth where I've lived and now will live once more. . . I've been to eternity and back. I know how the dead would feel to live again.
>
> CHARLES A. LINDBERGH
> *(on sighting Ireland after his solo Atlantic crossing in 1927)*

FROM FLIGHT
1927

Never in the history of aviation has a flying exploit so stirred the public imagination as the crossing of the Atlantic by Capt. Charles Lindbergh. Probably the nearest approach to it we have had in this country was the return of Hawker and Mackenzie Grieve from their Transatlantic attempt in 1919, when, after having been missing for a week, news was at last received that they had been picked up and were safe. Even the successful flight across the Atlantic, from Newfoundland to Ireland, by Alcock and Brown, in the same year, hardly aroused such wide spread interest and enthusiasm as that which found expression on Sunday last when, it is estimated, more than 100,000 people flocked to the Croydon aerodrome to see Lindbergh arrive from Brussels. That portions of the crowd broke through the flimsy barriers and swarmed on to the aerodrome is scarcely to be wondered at, nor should we blame too severely those who committed this breach of aviation etiquette. It is something to the good that the Londoner takes enough interest in flying to stream out to Croydon in his tens of thousands to see the hero of a famous flight. He cannot be expected, yet, to know that by getting on to the aerodrome he is not only endangering himself, but also the occupants of any aircraft that may be attempting to land there. As it was, we think it speaks well for a London crowd that Lindbergh's machine was not, by the irresistible crush, seriously damaged, and that the only repairs necessary before he was able to fly the "Spirit of St. Louis" to Gosport for dismantling, preparatory to sending it back to America, were a few patches of fabric here and there.

The Armstrong Whitworth Argosy. A specification was conceived originally in 1922 for the Empire routes pioneered by the Royal Air Force and pilots such as Alan Cobham. This biplane driven by three 420 hp Jaguar radial engines, proved unsuitable for the Empire routes when introduced in 1926. Passengers complained of noise and drafts, leaking roof panels and stiff necks from poor seat design.

56

By his flight Lindbergh has done one very great thing, as far as Great Britain is concerned. He has helped – even if it should prove only for a short period – to make the British people "air-minded". For that we cannot thank him enough.

DRAMATIC CROSS CHANNEL TEST
1929

Failure at 140 m.p.h.

There was witnessed recently an arduous test conducted in a fast plane to prove that Ku-bist Hair Fixative would indeed keep the speedman's hair in order under the most severe conditions. On the first trial, at Brooklands, speeds up to 70 m.p.h. failed to displace a single hair, and it was not until flying at 140 m.p.h. that the wind whipped the smoothly brushed locks into confusion.

Moral. – If you motor fast and bareheaded, let Ku-bist Hair Fixative keep your hair smooth and tidy all day.

At bath-time you can use Ku-bist Pine Tar Shampoo to remove the day's dust and bring back the Burnished glow of health to your hair.

LONDON TO BERLIN NON-STOP
1929
By Colonel L. A. Strange, D.S.O., M.C., D.F.C.

At Croydon Aerodrome, October 24, 06.30, a high southerly wind was blowing, which reached almost gale force with gusts of hard rain storms, when the "Spartan" was being run up on the tarmac. H. W. R. Banting, late 58 Squadron, and myself, late No. 5 Squadron, soon packed our suit cases (an extra 56 lbs) into the luggage locker, and off we went, hoping to reach Berlin non-stop in about six hours.

With 48 gallons of petrol we estimated to

have at least 18 gallons reserve, or 3½ to 4 extra flying hours in case of bad head wind.

The take-off was extremely good, except for a very soft spot just off the tarmac which pulled us up a bit and put our "tail well up." This came down again when we met the down draught from the hills and trees in the southwest corner of the aerodrome. A few minutes later we were well up and just under the clouds at 800 ft. Lympne was reached in fairly good time, in spite of the cross winds and hard rain.

The "Spartan" with her heavy load, was flying perfectly with the "Cirrus," Mark III, well throttled back to 1,800. Our compass crossing to Calais, allowing for the southerly wind, was only a few points off due south, and the crossing took about 20 mins. In view of the low visibility and clouds this bit of our trip was only pleasant to reflect upon when comparing it with the far more unpleasant experience of those people who seemed to prefer the high seas.

Our course then lay up the coast to Bray Dunes, the point where aircraft must cross the Franco-Belgian frontier on this route with the wind helping rather than otherwise we made very good time to Ostend, but with the clouds getting very much lower, about 200 ft.

This height enabled us to watch very clearly our friends the Belgians just waking up and taking their morning milk bottles from the doorstep. A little later when we began to bear eastward, the business people in Bruges were off to their work, and then Holland, the lowest-lying country in the world, the land of windmills and canals. Strips of tulip bed and black and white cows. Banting described this country as "unprintable" from 100 ft., but to me it was of vast interest in noting the method of the production of bulbs the growing of what appeared to be willows in very narrow strips for miles on end in wet looking country, and the particular care and small herds of black and white Fresian cattle and the various methods of agriculture.

I also noted that most of the small farms possessed a large brown dog, which appeared to greet us, either joyfully or as a noisy intruder on his slumbers. By 09.30 most of the high ground was beginning to connect with the clouds, and so on at 100 ft. past Hertogenbosch,

Arnhem on our right, then Zutphen, until on reaching the German frontier at Oldenzaal it became necessary to stick right on the railway to Bentheim. Our altimeter showing minus 100 ft. from Croydon aerodrome, and there being nothing to see between the clouds and house-tops it occurred to us that a canal, perhaps, would be less likely to have entered a tunnel suddenly than the railway.

As our interest in the countryside would have been interfered with by the pleasant pastime of cloud flying, we turned back and bore north into more low-lying country, and soon got back on to the Amsterdam-Hanover air route. Our course now being due E, took us N. of Rhine and Osnabruck, where the weather began to clear and improve rapidly, until at Minden, some-where about 10.30 we were flying at 3,000 ft. in beautiful weather, with a grand view of the Hartz mountains ahead to the S.E., and the busy town of the Schaumg beneath us, the big Steinhuder Meer with its island that looks like a boat in the middle down on our left, and the Ems-Weser Kanal stretching in blue ribbon from one horizon to the other.

This is good flying country, with the names of towns plainly written on the aerodromes, and smoke fires in the circle, and other things comforting to a pilot's eye and by the increasing number of machines passed and seen, aviation seemed, indeed, to be taken seriously round about Hanover which we were over about 11.00. Then came large tracts of forest country. Hereabouts the farmers seemed to be par-ticularly efficient, their corn stacks being beau-tifully thatched and in line, their cattle well cared for, indeed, agriculture appeared to be in a far better state than here at home. On we go over most interesting countryside and many large forests; across the Elbe running down past Magdeburg, we were soon close to Berlin, over the beautiful lake country, with Potsdam just down on our right, and "Berlin" in large white lettering showing up plainly from the air, on the Templehof aerodrome.

This appeared to be almost in the middle of Berlin, and looked about a mile long and nearly as wide, with lines of large hangars, and dozens of machines on the vast stretches of tarmac. As

Preparing for the Schneider Cup race in 1929, warrant officer Dan Molin, Italian pilot with his twin-engine Savoia Marchetti plane, the *Flying Egg,* in the then new hangar at Calshot.

THE LIGHT 'PLANE ALTITUDE RECORD

The Royal Aero Club announce that the height attained by Lady Heath (formally Mrs. S.C. Eliott-Lynn) on October 8 last on the Avro Avian was 5,268 m. (17,280 ft). This height is exactly the same as that accomplished by the Hon. Lady Bailey on a D.H. "Moth" on July 5 last. The altitude record for the Two-Seater Class Light Aeroplane is therefore still retained by the Hon. Lady Bailey.

METALS MAKE SPEED
by Professor A.M. Low

The coming of the aeroplane immensely stimulated the search for light metals that would bear equal strains with steel and iron. Aluminium is, as regards weight almost ideal metal, but unfortunately it is not suitable for most engineering purposes, in the pure form. A vast range of alloys have therefore been produced, with the result that we can have all-metal aeroplanes, much stronger than the wood and canvas structures of twenty years ago and weighing no more in proportion to size.

The same principles applied to other forms of transport, especially coupled with scientific streamlining, will work a revolution. An aluminium Normandie or Queen Mary is impracticable at the present time, chiefly on the grounds of cost. But there is also the fact that most aluminium alloys are eroded by sea water – a fact that prevented the use of aluminium in seaplane floats, until quite recently when an alloy that resisted the action was made.

This is not an advertisement for aluminium – I hold no shares in aluminium producing companies! It is merely pointing out that just as shedding a few pounds of fat increases the speed of a runner, so shedding a few pounds may increase the speed of transport. The revolution that is taking place may prove to be as important as that which took place when bronze and iron first began to take the place of stone.

MANY INVENTIONS
1932

In last week's *Aeroplane* a solemn warning was issued to African air mail pilots to beware of local hippopotami. One of these agile amphibians bit a large piece out of one of H.M. mail barges on the Zamboosi or some such streamlet. Pilots are asking how this occurrence is likely to affect them?

The question is: Has the African hippo changed his habits and diet? Are air-mail pilots to expect him to lurk in the topmost branches of Twangum trees and snatch frugal meals of fuselage from passing air-liners. Naturalists, as well as air pilots, are gravely concerned about it especially owing to the sinister report which has just come to hand that a bright red G.P.O. barge bearing urgent 'mails was recently attacked and sunk in the Manchester Ship Canal by a shoal of fresh-water prawns. The answer, in Africa at least, seems to be not to land on a hippodrome in error for an aerodrome and eschew low flying over the forests.

Amy Johnson (Mollison), formerly a typist from Yorkshire, who flew solo from England to Australia in 19½ days in 1930 in a De Havilland Moth to acclaim and celebrity. Her husband, James Mollison, made the first solo crossing of the Atlantic in a Puss Moth two years later. Formidable achievements for the light aeroplane of the period.

THE CAPE RECORDS SHATTERED AGAIN

Mrs. Amy Mollison's Triumph over Vicissitudes, 1936

By setting up two new air records on the London – Cape Town route, Mrs. Mollison has once again shown herself as probably the greatest airwoman in the world.

Tommy Rose, only a few months before, had apparently put the Cape record out of the reach of possible contenders for a long time to come. In the most graceful and easy way, Amy Mollison beat this record by over eleven hours.

The flight had started on Monday, May 4th, and by Wednesday she had flown 5,000 miles to Mossamedes, in Portuguese West Africa. To reach this point Mrs. Mollison had to make one hop of 1,800 miles, which was largely over the sea. She rested at Mossamedes for a few hours and then started out for Cape town, which was reached on Thursday at 3.31 p.m., after a flight of 3 days 6 hours and 26 minutes.

Mrs. Mollison rested for nearly three days before starting on the return Cape to London route. Her performance on the return flight was equally meritorious. Her overall time was 4 days 16 hours 16 minutes, showing a really remarkable gain of 1 day 14 hours 41 minutes on the previous record of 6 days 6 hours 57 minutes, also set up by Rose.

Some of the gigantic hops that Mrs. Mollison made on this journey are well worth noting, and comparison of her performance with that of the Imperial Airway liners which follow the same route is, if not absolutely fair, a striking proof of her endurance and navigating skill.

Starting from Cape Town at 9.28 p.m. on Sunday, Mrs. Mollison made a flight of 19 hours 12 minuets to Mpika, which she reached at 4.40 on Monday. The air liners take two days to arrive at Broken Hill, which is just south of this point, so that she travelled farther in one day than the liner does in two.

On the second day out from Cape Town Mrs. Mollison arrived at Juba, which put her one day in advance of Tommy Rose's record time. He had taken three days to reach Kisumu, considerably S.S.W. of Juba. On this lap Mrs. Mollison maintained, and even improved upon, her habit of averaging just double the speed of the air liners.

From Juba was made one of the most notable hops of all. Although she had only arrived during Tuesday afternoon, Mrs. Mollison started out for Khartoum at 4 a.m. next morning, reaching there at 9.20 a.m. After fuelling the 'plane, Mrs. Mollison continued towards Cairo,

having spent only one hour on the ground. Cairo was reached at 7.6 p.m. on Wednesday, the 1,050 miles from Khartoum having been completed in 20 hours 41 minutes. She was then one day ahead of the record, and had taken less than half the time of the airways.

Four thousand five hundred miles out of the total distance of 6,600 had been covered. Now began the journey to Europe, and, incidentally, into bad weather. By returning to England via Athens and Austria, Mrs. Mollison chose a different route from Flight-Lieut. Rose who went by Benghazi, Tunis and Cannes, but there is little advantage as far as distance is concerned between these two routes. En route for Athens the speed of the 'plane was reduced by head winds to 110 m.p.h., and some discomfort was caused by the lack of flying maps for that region. Greece was reached at about half-past ten on Thursday morning.

Still without proper flying maps she started out for England, but as she went on the weather became worse. Aided by an ordinary map of the route, she was able to pick out Graz, Austria, which she passed at 5.15 p.m. on Thursday. Farther north-east over the Alps conditions became very bad. Dense fog and violent storms made flight impossible, and so she was forced to retrace her steps and land at Graz.

The landing at Graz was made at 7.2 p.m., and thus she had been flying for two hours without getting any nearer to London. Next morning she left for Croydon which was reached in the afternoon at 1.35. A very early departure from Graz aerodrome was made impossible by the fogs which prevailed in the district.

Breaking records of this type does not merely ask for a thorough knowledge of aerial navigation and a strong constitution, but requires also many months of preparation and planning. Although the credit for the performance is Amy's, we must pay tribute, too, to the constructors of her Percival Gull, the Castrol organisation and others who helped to make the flight a possibility, and to those courteous individuals who gave valuable service by arranging landing facilities for her.

A promotion for Lignes Aériennes G. Latécoére. The massive French Latécoére *Lieutenant de Vaisseau Paris* carried away numerous records of the day in the ultra-marine heavy class.

CAPTAIN OF THE KING'S FLIGHT
1936

His Majesty The King has approved the creation of the new office of Captain of the King's Flight and Flight-Lieutenant E. H. Fielden, A.F.C., R.A.F.O., has been appointed to that office.

This, surely, is a sign of the times; and it affords further evidence of King Edward's very real interest in and practical appreciation of the value of aviation.

Another example of His Majesty's personal interest in flying was afforded on July 8th when, as head of the Royal Air Force, he flew to four R.A.F. stations on a tour of inspection, the first time in history that a reigning monarch had done such a thing.

Flight-Lieutenant Fielden, known to the R.A.F. as "Mouse" Fielden, who was personal pilot to the King when he was Prince of Wales, keeps the royal 'plane at Hendon.

When H.R.H. The Duke of Kent flies on matters of State, it is generally Flight-Lieutenant Fielden who pilots him.

MISS JEAN BATTEN'S GREAT ACHIEVEMENT
1936

In these days when one can seldom open a newspaper without reading of some aviator's narrow escape or thrilling episode, Miss Batten's uneventful flight from Lympne to Auckland comes as a pleasant change.

A famous Danish explorer once said that adventures were a sign of incompetence. Whether this is true or not Miss Batten's flight will be remembered as a fine example of careful planning and perfect navigation. As she herself said, "I have left nothing to chance and I have perfect confidence in the machine." She took off from Lympne on October 5th and landed in Auckland on the 16th, taking 11 days 2 hours for the whole journey, thus being the first to fly direct from England to New Zealand. During her flight she also broke the solo record for the journey from England to Australia by more than a day. The previous record of 6 days 21 hours was held by H. F. Broadbent. Miss Batten's trip consisted of nine well planned hops. The first day she arrived at Brindisi, the second Basrain, Iraq, the third at Karachi and on the fourth day she flew to Akyab in Burma. It was between Akyab and Singapore that she encountered the worst weather, but it did not hold up her progress to any great extent. On the whole she was very fortunate as regards the weather, and she had perfect conditions in crossing the Timor Sea on the sixth day. There was a delay at Sydney for a satisfactory weather report and after two days the State Meteorologist announced that there would be a following wind for the first 1,000 miles of her crossing. Conditions remained good over the Tasman Sea and she flew straight to Auckland, where she landed at 5.35 on Friday, October 16th, having made the crossing in record time. Incidentally she was also the first woman to make this crossing which is considered even more dangerous than an Atlantic flight, for over the Atlantic one is scarcely ever out of sight of a ship, while there are very few vessels journeying between Australia and New Zealand. In addition, there are not the regular and scientific weather reports which one has on the Atlantic, and storms are

apt to blow up very suddenly in mid-ocean.

The Australian Civil Aviation Board took a brave step in allowing Miss Batten to make this crossing in a single-engined plane, for had there been an accident the blame would have been on their shoulders. Miss Batten being successful, the Board can hardly prevent others from attempting the crossing which may soon become a regular service. Her machine , a Percival Vega Gull, fitted with a single Gipsy engine, lubricated with Wakefield Patent Castrol oil, and carrying 145 gallons of petrol, has a range of ten hours. When fully loaded the 'plane carried a weight of 2,950 lbs. It functioned perfectly throughout, and is another credit to British craftsmanship.

In her previous flights Miss Batten has always shown the same skill and care. In 1934 she flew from England to Auckland in fifteen days, and in the following year she was the first woman to complete the double journey from England to Australia and back. In the same year she flew from Lympne to Port Natal, her 61 hours 15 minutes beating Mrs. Mollison's previous best time. She was the first woman to fly the South Atlantic, and her time beat the existing record set up by Señor Compo, the Spanish airman.

Miss Batten has shown once again that women's flights are not matters of luck, and one is drawn to conclude that women have a special aptitude for these long-distance records.

Far Left: **Mexico, Central America and Havana timetables from the mid-30's.**

Air-minded Americans - an early 1930s brochure *Wings Over The Americas.* By the late 1920s the most influential trends in air liner design originated in the US.

THE KING'S CUP AIR RACE
1936

A splendid race despite terrible flying conditions

Jumping into first place at the ninth lap, Mr. Charles Gardner, in Sir Connop Guthrie's Percival Vega Gull hung on to his lead and won the King's Cup Air Race at 164.5 m.p.h.

The winner is a young pilot of 25 who was seventh in last year's race. Earlier in the year he flew to India and took part in the race for the Viceroy's Cup. In the King's Cup Race this year he was the only competitor who improved on the speed on which his handicap was based. His plane with a Gipsy engine using Patent Castrol oil, completed the course 3 m.p.h. faster than was estimated.

Flt.-Lt. Tommy Rose, last year's race winner, was second in Lady Wakefields' Hawk Six, and third place was taken by a new twin-engined high wing monoplane, Lord Willoughby de Broke's Double Eagle, flown by Flt. Lt. Wilson.

It was the fifteenth race for the Cup, and in many ways the most remarkable. The attendance at the aerodrome in the public enclosures was very poor, due largely to the appalling weather conditions. It rained the whole time; one competitor said flying was "like riding a bicycle without tyres down a flight of steps." Visibility was so poor that most of the pilots had to fly as low as 200 feet to enable them to see the pylons, and yet, no one was disqualified for cutting corners.

It was interesting to watch the different kinds of banking employed. The course was the shortest ever used in the race – 26 miles round and only one of the three turns was comfortably wide. Tommy Rose hugged the pylons, as though they were rails round the course, with throttle full out he banked vertically, sometimes going a fraction of a degree over the vertical. Mr. Falk, on the other hand, at first took a relatively wide sweep, swinging outwards as though attached to a piece of elastic. His flying was regular and accurate, but his wide turns lost him a few seconds and later he changed his technique and hung closely to the pylons.

The race was a triumph for Capt. G. W. Percival, who designed two machines, the winning Vega Gull and also the fastest machine in the race, the Duke of Kent's Percival Mew Gull, in which he himself completed the 300 mile course at 203 m.p.h. to be placed fourth. Mr. Percival, starting at scratch, flew high so that he could over-take the smaller machines. He must have had great difficulty in seeing the pylons in such weather conditions, but his times were

The endless quest for speed - the Supermarine Napier S.5. racing seaplane. The victorious Supermarine aircraft established British supremacy in the Schneider Trophy races.

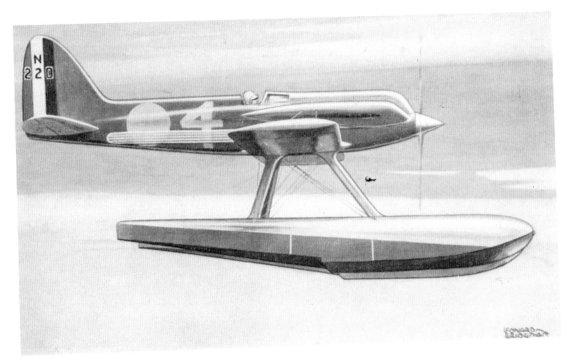

Publicity for a flying meeting in Basel in 1925. After World War I, there was an excess of pilots. Some, flying war-surplus aeroplanes, earned a hazardous living giving thrilling displays of stunt flying and wing-walking.

very regular and in his last round he broke the lap record; diving down to finish, he brought the speed up to 211 m.p.h. Mr. W. Dancy and Mr. F. W. Rowarth successfully solved the problem of handicapping. They estimated the speeds of fourteen planes so accurately that the finishing order was in doubt until the last moment.

In a flying sense the race was excellent. There was no failure in aircraft, engine or navigation. All the starters finished the course at full throttle, and there was little distance between the winner and the last man home.

AN AERIAL ASCOT
Flight, 1931

The Household Brigade Flying Club meeting held at Heston Air Park last Wednesday bids fair to become the chic social event of the season in the flying world.

Wednesday last July 22, presented a very animated spectacle to those who were fortunate enough to be invited to Heston. It was not a public function, in fact the general public were definitely discouraged by the aerodrome being advertised as being closed (whatever that may mean), but the number of visitors was quite large enough to make the show considerably more than a success.

Messrs. Norman and Muntz must, figuratively speaking, have rubbed their hands with glee when they saw so many of just the sort of people they set out to cater for gathered together on their aerodrome. Airwork, Ltd., have always made it their policy to encourage the people who consider themselves well up the social scale and who can afford more or less what they want in the way of aircraft, and by holding such functions as a meeting of the Household Brigade Flying Club at Heston large numbers of these are attracted and interested, with the eventual result, we hope, of their learning to fly and purchasing aircraft of their own. On this occasion the presence of H.R.H. The Prince of Wales set the seal of social success on the meeting, and we are all very grateful to him for coming. Just what it can have meant to him few will realise, but in view of the fact that during the morning of the same day he opened the Royal Welsh Agricultural Show at Llanelly, and that he flew from there to Heston in order to be present at this meeting, it will be seen that the debt of gratitude owed him for his part in furthering the cause of flying is very large indeed. The Prince of Wales with his characteristic thoroughness has not used aircraft to make his hard days easier, but has done so in order that he may cram still more public service into each twenty-four hours, and the way in which he does so should make any sceptic ashamed of his doubts as to the utility of aircraft, and will also make most men wonder what they were talking about

when they averred that they were so busy that they couldn't find time for this or that.

The Household Brigade Club would naturally collect unto themselves a galaxy of beauty on such an occasion and on our arrival we expected to see not only the latest fashions but also the right people wearing them; what we did

Rather social - Brooklands Club during the great days. C.G. Grey, founder of *The Aeroplane* and commentator on matters aeronautical, once wrote: "the spectators were very much like an Ascot crowd in sports clothes . . . with the Brigade of Guards' pilots there . . . aviation is obviously going to be the done thing".

Test flown at Brooklands in 1924, the Hawker single-seater fighter called the "Woodcock". A standard service aeroplane, carrying full military equipment, it showed the great advances in speed and manoeuvrability achieved in this type of aeroplane. This was the first of a long line of Hawker fighters that carried on the traditions set by the little Sopwith Tabloid of 1913.

69

A Zurich flying poster. Displays, races and exhibitions confirmed the theatrical nature of the aviation business, but public enthusiasm for flying was not always parallelled by support for scheduled commercial flights.

not anticipate was that we should see so many of the latest fashions or so much beauty. Bowler hats seem to have become the correct wear for male or female, and all shapes and sizes were to be seen. Personally we feel that those ladies who affected large brimmed hats gained the most comfort from the shade afforded, particularly when they gazed at the aircraft in the sky, but there is no denying that the bowler type is very attractive – husbands had better pawn theirs quickly until the fashion has passed if they want to retain them for themselves.

On the Prince of Wales' arrival, together with his equerry, in two Puss Moths, he was received by the President of the Club, Major-General C. E. Corkran, C.B., C.M.G., and at once evinced interest in the wide range of aircraft which had gathered at the meeting. It certainly was a representative gathering, and we do not remember ever having seen so many types together before. In all there was a total of over 80 aircraft spread about the aerodrome, with specimens of the Moth, Avian, Puss Moth, Wessex, Ford, Reid-Rambler, Arrow Active, Sikorsky, Avro 6, Klemm, Breda, Woodpigeon, Spartan Arrow, Autogiro, Bluebird, Civilian Coupe, Widgeon, Swift, Avro Tutor, Redwing, Martlet, Desoutter Monospar, Lincock, Willdhover, Veronca, while during the afternoon the Fairey Long Range machine flew over repeatedly and let us see her graceful lines, and Hadrian, built as the poultry fancier would say, "for utility more than for show," and consequently, not quite so graceful also heaved his bulk around and blotted out the sun. With regard to his activities we understand that he did sterling work on that day, as he was one of the aircraft to denude the British banks of somewhere above 25 tons of gold and to transfer it to France and Germany.

The programme was rearranged from the published form so people had to rely on the announcer for their knowledge of what was happening. This is really as it should always be, and we cannot help wondering why some people will continue to issue programmes for flying meetings which give a list of events and even the times at which they are supposed to start. By far the better way is just to give a list of events without any times, then to let the announcer do the rest.

The first item was the preliminary flights in the final of the "Gwynn Madocks" Cup. This is a landing competition held annually by the Household Brigade Club in which the competitors have to land as near the centre of the circle on the aerodrome as they can, from a height of 500 ft., without using their engine. The member obtaining the most marks in three attempts being winner. The final flight was the last item on the programme, and resulted in a win for Capt. J. Harrison with 155 marks, L. Grey Sykes being second with 104 and Capt. J. Hargreaves third with 52 marks. At the end of the programme the Prince of Wales graciously presented the cup to the winner.

Flt. Lt. Rawson then showed off the Autogiro demonstrating the way it can be landed almost vertically, and he was followed by Flt. Lt. Stainforth on an Avian. Stainforth's aerobatics are now well known, and the steady way in which he rolls, loops and bunts is an education for the less experienced pilots who think that looping consists of pulling the stick back hard and hoping for the best. Following this came the Spartan Arrow flown by Col. Strange, and known as the slowest flying English light aircraft; by that we do not mean that it does not go fast as well, but that it is perfectly controllable at lower speed than most others.

O. McKenna put up a very fine show on the Lincock; this machine was fitted for inverted flying, and therefore able to do such things as vertically banked turns when upside down, which are naturally impressive. He shows that he has learnt the art of showmanship as well as aerobatics, as his manoeuvres were all well out over the aerodrome and sufficiently high to be safe.

This advertising dates from 1929. The plane is a Ford Tri-Motor - during the 1920s it was used for ambulance work, crop dusting and freight carrying, and an ever-growing variety of jobs.

71

DUNCAN DAVIS,
Brooklands School of Flying,

Brooklands was the first aerodrome in Great Britain and the home of many famous air pioneers. From its inception it collected inside the famous Race Track men and women who were out for one thing and one thing only – the Conquest of the Air.

Should you join us – help us to turn you out a pilot worthy of our traditions and standards.

HOW AND WHERE TO LEARN TO FLY
by William Court, the famous Aeronautical Correspondent and Publicist, 1937

The new season opens with the prospects for the air pilot as bright or indeed brighter than they have ever been. If you were to look through the books of the Guild of Air Pilots and Air Navigators of the British Empire, for instance – the body which looks after the status and employment of the professional pilot – you would find they have no one who is unemployed.

In fact, both they and the air line operators are searching frantically for experienced pilots to man the air liners which need them. Pilots are at a premium.

Those anxious to learn to fly, with a view to becoming professional pilots and commanders of the giant flying boats of Imperial Airways, cannot do better than take the long course at the Air University known as Air Services Training, Ltd., of Hamble, Southampton.

This course lasts about three years and costs up to £850. It is, however, the most complete aeronautical training in the world; and Imperial Airways employ those students who pass the course satisfactorily at this University.

Thorough Training

Pupils are given a thorough training not only in air pilotage but also in engineering, air navigation, wireless, and all other subjects on which Imperial Airways require Certificates and Licences to be secured. Even training on flying boats is included and this cannot be secured elsewhere. It is, of course, vital for those contemplating duties as flying boat pilots. Although £850 is a lot to find, when one considers that it includes 300 hours of flying, the course is really remarkably cheap. Residential accommodation is also available, with facilities for every game.

There will, of course, be many who cannot afford £850 for training, although this fee is no more than training for medicine might involve. Emoluments in return can reach £1,500 per annum for the best pilots at the top who will one day command ocean-going flying boats. For those of more modest means there are many other schools at which tuition can be given.

The youngster, for instance, can be sent to the College of Aeronautical Engineering at Chelsea for two or three years. For quite modest fees he can receive all necessary training in engines, etc. This College works in liaison with Brook1and's School of Flying and the pupils pass there for their flying training.

Brooklands

Brooklands itself, one of the nurseries of flying in the world, offers, of course, the best class of training for both the amateur "A" and the commercial "B" Licences. Here the pupil can learn by practical work in the hangars all about aero engines and can work on actual engines used in the school machines. A course for the training, up to the 100 hours' solo stage required for the "B" Licence, would not cost more than £200. The pupil can live quite cheaply in the quarters available at Brooklands and for £2 weekly his room and food can all be paid for. The keen student will secure his "A" Licence within three weeks, his "B" Licence within six months and for the rest of his first year he can go on piling in solo cross-country experience in all weathers. This is vital if he is to attract a nice job as a commercial pilot.

No air line could entrust an aircraft full of passengers to a pilot with less than 500 hours' hard solo experience, and most demand 1,000 hours. The best way to put in this time, either at Brooklands or elsewhere, is to buy a second-hand aeroplane, such as a BA "Swallow" hand monoplane or a Gipsy Moth biplane. About £400 to £500 would have to be expended, but at the end of the year's hard flying the machine would fetch back as much of this capital as it cost. Second-hand aeroplanes have a way of keeping their market value up year by year. Flying tuition, which costs 30s. an hour for solo flying round an aerodrome in school or club machines, costs only 10s. per hour once you use your own machine. The costs are confined to fuel and oil and the usual 25 hours' long checks and overhauls.

The 500 hours of solo would then cost no more than £250, and the £500 of capital expended on the aircraft would be recovered at the end of it all.

Navigation

Navigation training at school lectures at Brooklands follows, and then navigation training in the air. This is easily picked up, and the pupil within a few weeks will find himself flying on long cross-country journeys alone with map and compass: studying winds and weather which

Deutsch Lufthansa was formed in 1926 with monopoly rights. It built airports and soon became the most efficient of the European airlines under the central direction of Erhard Milch, Goering's deputy, and the most important name in German post-war aviation, both military and civil.

This superb study is from the *Illustrated London News* archives. The struggle of the first commercial airline companies in Britain ended in 1924 when the Government formed Imperial Airways. By 1927 Imperial had spread its wings as far as Basra, at the head of the Gulf, and survey flights had reached India.

73

Curtiss Flying Service - Glenn Curtiss, of Harvard USA, was, between 1901-1909, a member of the Canadian inventor Alexander Bell's Aerial Experiment Association. In 1910 he made the first flight from the deck of a ship, a US cruiser.

are all so necessary for his training. A "blind flying" course should be taken after 300 hours' solo have been put in, and then the pupil should fit blind flying instruments to his own machine and keep practising cloud flying. Flights abroad should be made frequently to learn the procedure of foreign touring and to acquire some knowledge of the air routes to the Continent

Within 12 months a keen student can have acquired, for an expenditure of not more than £500, his "A" and "B" Flying Licences, his 2nd Class Navigator's Ticket, and his G.P.O. Wireless Licence. Within two years, having 500 hours to his credit, he should have obtained his Ground Engineer's Certificate, and be proficient in instrument flying.

This works out at only £1 an hour less than joy-riding charges. He will be fully fledged on this to secure employment. It is much the cheapest way of doing things. There are many schools round London, of course, where training of a thorough nature to "B" Licence standard can be acquired for £200, or perhaps even less. Aircraft Exchange and Mart, for instance, run a very efficient school at Hanworth Airport, Feltham, off the Great West Road. At Heston Airport, on the other side of the road, Airwork, Ltd., the owners, run their own school and specialise particularly in navigation. For those living on the South side of London there is the Redhill School of Flying and Air Travel, run by Mr. Fred Holmes at the new Gatwick Airport. At Croydon Airport there is Surrey Flying Services Ltd., one of our oldest schools; here, too, will be found Croydon Airways, both of whom specialise in this tuition. In the North-East there is the Herts. and Essex Aero Club, very live and up to date at Broxbourne, while on the North the famous De Havilland firm have their own Flying school at Hatfield where pupils actually learn how to construct an aeroplane which year by year they enter in the King's Cup Air Race. Here an apprentice scheme has been evolved where the pupil may attend school for about two years. The premium is £250 and at the end of the period the best brains are taken on as designers if the pupils do not go on to flying. The London Aeroplane Club also lives at Hatfield. Associated with Brooklands are the Clubs at Brighton

Airport and at Northampton, as well as the Cinque Ports Flying Club at Lympne. At Gravesend and Rochester, for those who live in these districts, similar tuition and training can be received and, generally speaking, London provides opportunity at most points of the compass.

There will be many who may be desirous of learning to fly "just for fun," or with a view to joining the R.A.F reserve, or to become private owners. The Light Aeroplane Clubs referred to cater for these. The course lasts only about three weeks, given suitable weather and costs the pupil no more than from £25 to £50, dependent on his own ability and on how quickly he is launched solo. After three hours' solo the coveted Licence is secured and only three hours' flying per year is necessary to renew it. But here again, the pupil who wants to fly a lot, or to own a machine, would be well advised to buy a second-hand machine early in his training so that he can learn cross-country flying and add to his solo experience in the cheapest possible way.

75

Open cockpit fun. The development of the small fast aeroplane in the 20s was encouraged by air racing, such as the Pulitzer Trophy races in America and the Schneider Trophy, and led directly to the modern fighter.

CLIPPED WINGS
By P. A. Turner, 1938

**Who describes the conditions
and machines peculiar to
Air Racing in America,
Which has Achieved immense
popularity in recent years**

Have you ever seen those pictures of American motor racing in which the air seems full of flying cars and drivers, with a couple disappearing over the edge of the banking? Well, American air racing is the same, only more so. This is shown only too well by the fact that five of the nine men who have succeeded in winning the Thompson Trophy, the most important race of the year, have since been killed.

Race meetings are held all over the country, the events being from scratch over courses ten miles or so in length which have to be lapped ten, twenty, or thirty times. The fleet of racing planes, generally about fifteen in number, are very evenly matched, and the racing is often exceedingly close.

The most important meeting of the year is the Cleveland National air races a three-day event held in September, which draws a crowd of eighty thousand or so every day. As well as the races, there are displays by the Services, aerobatic displays given by American and Continental pilots, and demonstrations of new 'planes.

The three chief races are the Bendix Trophy, the Greve Trophy and the Thompson Trophy. The Bendix Trophy is a trans-Continental race from Los Angeles to Cleveland. The past two events have been dominated by the new Severesky P-35 fighters, which are now being supplied to the U.S. Army Air Corps. They are low wing, all-metal monoplanes with Pratt & Whitney Twin Wasp 1,000 h.p. engines, and one of their special features is the use of liquid-tight compartments in the wings for carrying the fuel, there being no separate petrol tanks. In '37, Frank Fuller, a wealthy sportsman, was the pilot of the winning Severesky, but this year he had to be content with second place, Miss Jacqueline Cochrane bringing another Severesky home in first place at an average speed of 249.77 m.p.h. She flew at 15,000 feet for most of the way and rarely saw the ground. The take-off is usually the most trying part of this race for the pilot, for the 'planes are overloaded with two hundred or more gallons of petrol in an effort to avoid a refuelling stop. One pilot had to enter his cabin bi-plane via the window owing to the space taken up by the

fuel tanks, and the previous year one of the machines had developed such a bad sway on its take-off run, that a tyre had ripped off and nosed over. By some miracle it did not go up in flames. It was in this race in 1936 that two well-known pilots had narrow escapes from a sticky ending.

Benny Howard and his wife were flying his well-known high wing cabin monoplane, "Mr. Mulligan," when one of the metal blades of the airscrew flew off into space. The vibration of the unbalanced engine was so great the 'plane got completely out of control and crashed, seriously injuring both occupants. Joe Jacobson, piloting Gar Wood's Northrop Gamma, was also going well when he suddenly felt a smashing blow and lost consciousness. When he came to a few seconds later, he found himself descending rapidly earthwards minus his aeroplane, little pieces of which were fluttering around him. He pulled the rip cord of his parachute and made a good landing, but the only part of his 'plane he could find was a foot of wing tip. Why the 'plane exploded is not known for certain.

The Louis W. Greve Trophy is a pylon race open to planes with engines of 550 cubic inches or less (about nine litres). The course is ten miles in length and rectangular in shape, with two long legs and two short, and has to be lapped twenty times. The 'planes themselves are amazing creations, and largely account for the high death roll. One might compare their constructors with the same kind of people who built Shelsley Specials in England, for the machines are just what one would imagine an aerial Bolster Special would be like. It is interesting to compare a Folkerts or Keith Rider Special with the Percival Mew Gull, the nearest approach to a racing 'plane we have in this country. The Folkerts Special, with which the late Rudy Kling swept the board at the 1937 Cleveland meeting and later met his death at Miami, has a supercharged six–cylinder Manasco engine developing 250 h.p., compared to the 224 h.p. of the Mew Gull's Gipsy 6, and weighs 1,385 lbs. fully loaded, compared to the 2,125 lbs. of the Mew Gull. It will, therefore, be seen that the Ameri-

This flying poster from 1924 depicts a floatplane. The word "seaplane" was first introduced by Sir Winston Churchill in 1913.

Another Gordon Bennett poster. The first Gordon Bennett balloon race was held in 1906 and the wealthy US enthusiast also presented trophies for international motoring competition.

can 'plane has more horse power and less weight, which goes a long way to explain why it does 308 m.p.h., compared to the Mew Gull's 250 m.p.h. Another important difference between the two is that the Folkerts has only 50 square feet of wing to carry it instead of the Mew Gull's 80 square feet. The main wing is an exceedingly thin plywood-covered fin mounted high up on the fuselage.

Great care is taken by the constructors of these ships to obtain a smooth surface, the general procedure being to emery paper the wing, then paint it and then wax it. The result of all this is a shimmering little creation with a main wing like a tail 'plane, and which needs over a mile run on the ground before it can take off. Weight being all-important, strength is cut down to the bare minimum, and there have been many cases of 'planes collapsing in mid-air. Especially was this the case in the past when eight, or even five-mile, circuits have been used, for these put a very great strain indeed on the "Half Pint" races.

Lee Miles lost his life in the '37 races when a wire broke on his wire-braced 'plane, with the result that the ship just fell apart in mid-air, both wings tearing off and striking the tail. Before Miles could switch off, the fuselage began to spin round on its own axis and continued some way in this fashion, only diving to the ground when the engine stopped. At another meeting a pilot lost his wings at a low altitude, but was able to "zoom" the 'plane up to a sufficient height on its engine alone, and made a successful parachute jump.

The Thompson Trophy is held over the same course as the Greve Trophy, but this year was increased to 300 miles and is open to 'planes of any capacity. This year's race saw a colossal battle between Roscoe Turner's Turner Laird Meteor and Erl Ortman's Keith Rider. Ortman shot into the lead at the start, with Turner sitting right on his tail. Last year, Turner lost this race when he cut a pylon and made a 360 degree to take it, and this year history repeated itself, but it was Ortman who cut the pylon and lost first place. Try as he could, he could not catch Turner, whose mid-wing monoplane had the twin Wasp Senior instead of the slightly smaller

twin Wasp Junior fitted to the Keith Rider, and the gallant Roscoe swept over the line in first place, having averaged 282 m.p.h. for the last few laps.

The four fastest 'planes in American racing are Roscoe Turner's Turner Laird, which is a mid-wing monoplane with a 14-cylinder Pratt and Whitney Twin Wasp Senior 14-cylinder engine, developing 1,000 h.p. at 2,300 r.p.m. The fuselage is covered with sheet metal from nose to trailing edge, and plywood aft to the trailing edge. The wing is also plywood-covered, and all control hinges are fitted with ball bearings. The undercarriage is non-retractable. The maximum speed is well over the 300 mark.

Howard Hughes' special 'plane, which broke the land speed record with a speed of 352 m.p.h., and still holds the trans-Continental record from east to west with a time of seven hours, 28 minutes, 25 seconds, is a low-wing monoplane with an all-metal fuselage and a Twin Wasp Senior engine. The all-wood wing was covered with inch thick plywood which was then shaved down to a quarter of an inch, polished, painted and waxed. It has two wings, a short and stubby one, with which it took the speed record, and a long and thin one, with which it took the trans-Continental record. It is now being investigated by the Army Air Corps.

Erl Ortman's Keith Rider, which was built for the MacRobertson race to Australia, but crashed in practice, killing its pilot, has since been rebuilt twice and is now very fast indeed. It is a low-wing monoplane with a Twin Wasp Junior engine and a retractable undercarriage. The fuselage is of metal and the wings wood-covered. It has finished second in the Thompson Trophy three years running, in '36 at 245 m.p.h., in '37 at 253 m.p.h., and in '38 at 282.69 m.p.h. Steve Wittman's Oshkosh Chief is the only 'plane with a water-cooled motor competing these days. It is very long and slim and very hard on the eye, a mid-wing monoplane with a Curtiss Conqueror engine and a wire-braced wing. Air reaches the radiator via a hole in the out-size in propeller spinners, which also contains several fan blades to blow air through the hole. The undercarriage is a strip of ⅜-inch thick sheet metal with a wheel at each end and the middle attached to the fuselage.

79

Aeroplanes for all - the most famous small biplane ever built, the De Havilland Tiger Moth. Introduced in 1925, Geoffrey De Havilland wanted a name and not a number for his aeroplane. "It suddenly struck me that the name Moth was just right . . . easy to remember, and might well lead to a series of Moths, all named after British insects" he said.

BEHIND THE SCENES IN THE RUNNING OF A FLYING CLUB.
By Duncan Davis
(Managing Director of the Brooklands Flying Club), 1937

An aeroplane is such an ordinary sight nowadays that it no longer rouses any particular interest, although it is noticeable that the average person does give a casual glance in the direction of a passing machine, which is more than he or she affords to other types of vehicles, except, perhaps, express trains.

There are flying clubs and schools all over the country at which machines are daily seen at work, rising and descending with almost monotonous regularity. So regularly, in fact, that those not 'in the know' may well come to the conclusion that the only two items necessary to keep a machine in the air are a pilot and a supply of petrol.

There is far more in it that this however, so let us take a peep behind the scenes at any well-run flying club and examine what goes on there.

Preparations

Preparations for the day's flying start at the close of that of the previous day. As soon as the machines are all on the ground they are wheeled across to the petrol pumps and their tanks replenished with petrol and oil. Following this, they are taken into the main hangars and any minor fault which may have become apparent during the day's flying is immediately rectified.

Next morning, whilst those who intend flying during the day are still in bed, the mechanics, or to give them their correct title, ground engineers arrive at the aerodrome and set to work on the machines. These men are all experts, and having passed their examinations, are licensed by the Air Ministry for their particular jobs. Some specialise in engines, and some on "airframes," as the main structure of the aeroplane is technically named. Let us first of all go round the machine with the airframe expert.

He starts by making a careful examination of all fabric – covered surfaces, i.e., the wings, tailplane rudder, etc., looking for tears which may have been caused by flying stones being knocked up by

the wheels, repairing any found. He will then inspect all moveable parts in connection with the control surfaces, and, where necessary, will grease them. The control cables will next be looked at for fraying or rust, and the working of the controls tested to see there is no stiffness anywhere. If there is, the cause must be found before the machine takes the air. The aeroplane being a biplane, he will next turn his attention to the wing bracing wires, seeing that they are at the correct tension, and that they are properly locked in position. If these wires show signs of slackness it may mean that a 'heavy' landing has 'pulled' a fitting, and this must be looked into.

Having examined the petrol tank for leaks, and the propeller for splits, the 'G.E.' next turns his attention to the undercarriage of the machine. The tyres will be examined for cuts, and their pressure checked; the wheels cleaned and greased, and their attachment to the axle checked over. The shock absorbers are tested, and the plates which fasten the undercarriage to the fuselage longerons are examined for any movement which may have occurred. This can usually be detected by the cracking of paint, and if this is so, should be closely investigated, in case a crack has occurred in the longerons at that point. Attention is then given to the tail skid and its attachment; the coil spring must be examined in case it has become stretched, and the check cable examined.

In Completion

Finally, he will get into the cockpits and examine the seats of the machine at the points where they are fastened to the fuselage members, to satisfy himself that all is correct there. Whilst inside he will inspect the longerons – that is, the main frame of the fuselage – with an electric torch, again to see that there are no cracks in the wood. Having eased his mind on these points, he will get out of the machine, and having taken a look at the ends of the wing spars will open the wings and lock them in position. His inspection of the machine is then complete.

The Engine

Whilst he has been doing this, the other 'G.E.', the engine expert, will not have been idle. Firstly, he will have taken off the engine cowl-

GERMAN AIRWAYS
DAILY CONNECTIONS EXCEPT SUNDAYS
TO AND FROM
AMSTERDAM · BERLIN · BREMEN · COLOGNE
DORTMUND · DÜSSELDORF · ESSEN · FRANCFORT
HALLE/LEIPZIG · HAMBURG · HANNOVER
MOSCOW · MUNICH

ing, and closely examined the cylinder heads of the motor for cracks, chaffing, etc. These things sometimes occur in the best of engines, and it takes an expert eye to see them. Marks which the layman would take for specks of dirt and scratches are diagnosed by the 'G.E's.' eye as cracks, and off comes that particular cylinder head, another being fitted in its place. Then he will take a look at the valve tappets, adjusting, if necessary, and turning the engine over compressions will see that all are good and equal. Any weakness is looked into, and, if necessary, off comes another head for inspection. The contact breakers of the magneto are cleaned and reset, the petrol filters cleaned, and the flow checked. Finally, he warms up the motor, eventually 'running it up' to see that it is giving full revolutions on each of the two magnetos (two sets of plugs being compulsory on all aircraft used for tuition or hire) and that the oil pressure is correct and steady. If it is too high, too low, or should waver then there is another investigation. The correct functioning of the instruments are also checked.

Deutsch Luft Hansa - in 1930 the German airlines carried 93,126 passengers. The 1930 routes of the Empire services of Imperial Airways measured 23,005 miles, not significantly longer than the German airlines although that nation had no empire at all.

81

International flying meeting at Zurich 1932. Public support for aerial derbys and their like was not unanimous. In 1927 in the English seaside resort of Bournemouth a pilot was angrily shot at for flying over the seafront. (There was a successful move-ment in Britain against flying competitions on Sundays.)

An alarming "Fright" service is advertised. Three types of aircraft, used by SCADTA on the Columbia rivers in the 1920s are shown: Dornier Wal and Merkur and Junkers F.13.

82

CROYDON IN SIX DAYS
PREVIOUS RECORD BEATEN BY 88 HOURS
1937

Remarkable Endurance

At 3.23 p.m., on Saturday, November 20th, Flying Officer A. E. Clouston and Mrs. Kirby-Green landed at Croydon, having completed the 14,700-mile round journey Croydon – Cape Town – Croydon in a few hours under six days.

Thus, in a flight which was remarkable for the machine's singular freedom from mechanical trouble, the amazing endurance shown by the flyers, and, above all, Flying Officer Clouston's exceptional navigating skill, no less than 88 hours were clipped from the previous record set up by Miss Amy Johnson.

The Comet aeroplane used is a four-years-old machine, fitted with two modified Standard Gipsy S4 Series II engines, with a cruising speed of approximately 200 m.p.h. and a fuel load of 264 gallons, and the performance of the machine itself is made even more remarkable by reason of the fact that the short notice at which the flight was arranged left little time for preparation.

Just how little attention to the machine was actually required during the flight may be judged from the brief halts made especially for the purpose; 30 minutes at Johannesburg, 33 minutes at Kisumu, 20 minutes at Khartoum, and under half-an-hour at Marseilles.

Cairo – Non-stop

On the outward journey, the weather remained consistently good, and the 2,300-mile flight from Croydon to Cairo was made non-stop.

It was hard luck that no less a time than seven hours should have had to be spent on the ground at the next stop at Khartoum, where some difficulty was experienced in obtaining the necessary permission to fly over the Sudd.

Cape Town was reached in 45 hours 2 minutes, beating Miss Amy Johnson's time by around 33 hours.

On the return flight, ice formation proved the worst threat to the machine, choking the vents of the fuel tank, but, fortunately the machine was fitted with an auxiliary vent in the cockpit which enabled the pilots to overcome the trouble.

The caption to this 1919 photograph reads "Paris Air 'Special' starts. International flying was inaugurated today with the departure of a 'special' to Paris from Hounslow". The customs office grants the pilot clearance.

Head Winds

Heavy head winds over the Mediterranean also caused trouble and considerably reduced the speed of the machine, necessitating a call for fuel at Marseilles; on this part of the journey the endurance of the pilots was tested to the uttermost limit (by this time they were physically tired out.)

Despite these difficulties, the flyers reached Croydon in 57 hours 23 minutes 39 hours less than the time taken by Brook, who held the previous record for this trip at 96 hours 20 minutes.

The total time for the journey was 5 days 17 hours 28 minutes, the average speed being a fraction under 190 m.p.h.

THE STORY OF A GREAT ADVENTURE
Review of Last Flight – The Story of Amelia Earhart's Tragic Round-The-World Flight 1938

"This is not a chronicle of regret, but of high and happy adventure. That is as she would have her book. May its pages convey some measure of the pervading charm and magic character of Amelia Earhart whose explorings were as much of the mind and spirit as of the air."

In this manner, Mr. George Palmer Putnam introduces the book, "Last Flight." The sentiments he expresses are borne out throughout the pages of what is undoubtedly a book to be read and re-read, a book which gives the reader an insight not only into the multitudinous activities and anxieties of a pioneer, but to a marked extent in the early chapters at least, the personality of Miss Earhart.

Mexican Flight

Much of the value of the book lies in the fact that it not only relates the highly interesting adventures of a pioneer whom we knew as an intrepid and courageous flyer, but that it gives us an insight into the personality of Miss Earhart herself – a personality which is as full of interest and charm as is the story of her adventures.

Here we are enabled to discover just how likeable that personality was.

Above all, Miss Earhart was gifted with a sense of humour unique in femininity; a virtue which apparently helped her more than a little throughout her career – whether in tight corners in the air, or in what otherwise might be embarrassing, and even daunting situations when she reached good solid earth.

Sopwith Hawker single-seater biplane, built for the 1919 Schneider Trophy, is seen at Brooklands. Great rivalry developed between the two principal contestants, Great Britain and Italy, for the prize. For the early 20th-century Italian artists the aeroplane became a sort of mechanical angel inspiring two new genres of art: aeropainting and aeropoetry.

84

For instance, after her Mexican flight, she landed at Newark. "In due course I was rescued. . . By husky policemen, one of whom in the ensuing melee took possession of my right arm and another of my left leg. Their plan was to get to the shelter of a near-by police car. . . . But their execution lacked co-ordination. For the armholder started to go one way, while he who clasped my leg set out in the opposite direction. . . . But, at that it was fine to be home again."

In many pages of the book one is delighted with her whimsical style, yet nowhere does she lose sight of her aims and ambitions.

Determination

Her determination too, is strong and persistent in her writings. For Amelia Earhart was first and foremost a woman determined that her sex should at length reach complete and undeniable emancipation. "I for one hope for the day when women will know no restrictions because of sex. " And again, when she was asked "Why are you attempting this round-the-world flight?" she answered "Because I want to . . . Here was a shining adventure, beckoning with new experiences, adding knowledge . . . Then, too, there was my belief that now and then women should do for themselves what men have already done – and occasionally what men had not done, thereby establishing themselves as persons, and, perhaps, encouraging other women towards greater independence of thought."

Few women of modern times can have had such a broad outlook on the problems of femininity as did Miss Earhart. Few women have the same determination or courage to lead the way to freedom as she endeavoured to do.

Search for Knowledge

But her concern for her fellow-sex did not blind her to the other, and possibly greater, problems of her flights.

Always she wanted to learn something new.

"But rather than focusing on the problem of making to-morrow's 'planes bigger and faster, I for one should like to see the technical genius develop a 'plane that could actually stay in the air while moving, perhaps, only 40 miles per hour, which I think can come without sacrificing top speeds, size or comfort."

In these days it is easy to be confused into believing that high speed are the only speeds of importance. Miss Earhart, in these few words, reminds us that is not so, and proves that she herself, a true pioneer, did what she did for the sake of the advancement of humanity, and not for any personal pleasure to be derived from flying faster or farther than anyone had ever previously flown.

Moreover, she fully realised the risk she ran. "Please don't be concerned. I've weighed it all carefully. With it (her world flight) behind me life will be fuller and richer. I can be content." "When I go," she often said, "I'd like best to go in my 'plane, quickly."

So, although the world is the poorer for the loss of a brave and charming personality, we who read "Last Flight" can be glad that the book stands out as one more of her many and lasting achievements. For in its pages are not only the chronicles of the adventure and dangers which beset the pioneer, the disappointments, the hard work, the tribulations and the joys, but a lesson to all who live to create, rather than to enjoy the creations of others. And for this the book should be read by everybody.

Romance above the clouds - the craze for flying spread across the social scale. "Be Up To Date and Aviate" was a slogan of the day, and aerial derbys in Britain were attended by members of the royal family and both Houses of Parliament.

This Swiss poster dates from 1937. Switzerland produced her own first aeroplane in the Dufaux biplane which flew across Lake Geneva on August 28, 1910.

IV. INTERNATIONALES 23. JULI – 1. AUG. 1937 FLUGMEETING ZÜRICH

Air Records and Record Breakers
by Robert Polendine, 1939

There are various ways in which you may set up a flying record of sorts. You may be the first crooner to fly upside down for five minutes non-stop, or an airline pilot streaking across the Channel with a fifty miles an hour tail wind. Either way you may put up a unique performance. But the real records are not so easy to come by, nor are they quite so spectacular as their name implies. These are the aeronautical achievements – including lighter as well as heavier-than-air craft – which are recognized by the Fédération Aéronautique Internationale. This body is the only authority in world aeronautics whose authority, probably because it has no political significance, is universally accepted. No record can be regarded as a *fait accompli* until it has been homologated by the F.A.I.

At the moment there are some 200 records which have official recognition though about fifty minor ones will disappear from the list on April 1st of this year. Of the remainder, only

about half a dozen are of popular interest; setting up a major record – particularly an absolute speed attempt – quickens the imagination more readily than an apparently pedestrian climb to 10,000 metres with a 1,000 kilograms load. But most records are simply "handicap" results in effect achieved within the limits of the class and category laid down by the F.A.I. and it is to the distribution of these minor distinctions, as well as the better known ones, that we must look for indications of the avenues of research which are engaging the attentions of the world's air powers at present.

Classification is according to the type of aircraft employed – aerostat (both balloon and dirigible), landplane, marine aircraft, amphibian, glider, motor glider, helicopter and even model aeroplane. The only type whose existence the F.A.I. steadfastly refuses to acknowledge is the autogiro.

The record requirements are divided into three broad categories – speed, distance and altitude – these are sub-divided into speed in a straight line and closed circuit, unladen and carrying specified loads, distance in a straight line, and closed circuit, and altitude laden and unladen. There are additional sub-divisions for women pilots and 21 "point-to-point" long-distance records. The so-called "absolute" records for speed, distance and altitude are included under their respective categories, but are distinguished by the award of a special diploma.

With a few unimportant exceptions the records are shared, as one would expect, by the leading Powers – Britain, France, Germany, Italy, Russia and the United States. Their detail distribution is very interesting.

From 1906, when Dumont put up the first official landplane record of 25.5 m.p.h., to 1935, this distinction only left France four times when the United States captured it for brief intervals. Then Wurster went out for it with the BF-113R at Augsberg and the record went to Germany at nearly 380 m.p.h. Udet, in the Heinkel He, has since pushed it up to nearly 400 m.p.h. over 100 kilometres, which means that any hopeful competitor will have to conjure up more than a comfortable margin over the existing *vitesse sur base* record before he begins to have a chance

88

A 1925 Bristol "Bloodhound" Type 84, with a Jupiter IV engine. A family business, BAC (British Aeroplane Company) also came to be known to stand for "Brothers and Cousins".

against the Heinkel. True, the 100 kms. record was set up at a higher altitude than the requisite 50 metres limit for *"sur base"* attempts, but there seems little doubt that the Heinkel and Messerschmidt are going to prove obstinate record-holders.

Marine Design Supreme

Before landplane speeds began to get really high, marine design had been stimulated by the now lamentably defunct Schneider Trophy contest, and in the "absolute" class seaplanes were unchallenged. The culmination of some intensive rivalry between the two countries finally left Britain with the Trophy and Italy with the record – gained three years after the last contest by Agello in the Fiat-engined Macchi Castoldi. This 440 m.p.h. record is still unbeaten after four years. One wonders whether the mysterious ultra-fast machine rumoured to be taking shape at Heston will take up the challenge. At the moment the only speed record reasonably within reach seems to be the landplane one if a little extra urge can be imparted to the "Spitfire" by a variable-pitch airscrew.

Italy holds most of the palms to-day in the speed categories, her indefatigable record breaker, Mario Stoppani, and Fiat engines sharing the credit between them. The same pilot, accompanied by Carlo Tonini, set up the existing closed-circuit seaplane record in the three-engined (Alfa-Romeo) Cantz in May, 1937. Italy's only other rivals here are the Soviet Union and – to a lesser degree – France, whose massive Latécoére *Lieutenant de Vaisseau Paris* has carried away most of the records in the ultra-heavy marine class.

Britain's Part

It will be noticed that Great Britain's name is conspicuously absent from "those mentioned" in connection with these records. It is not until we consider the "point-to-point" category that British aviation begins to give a true account of itself, probably because this is the most promising field for non-Government inspired efforts. Most of the records which have come our way in recent years have been due to private enterprise. The Long Range Development Unit's feat and "Mercury's" hop to the Cape are, of course, exceptions.

89

This flying meeting of 1931 promised aerobatics. Elements popular in the earliest days, such as barnstorming (i.e. itinerant exhibition flying) and comic turns, had largely been dropped by this time.

New York Airways was a subsidiary of Pan American, and in 1931 was sold to Eastern Transport. They employed Ford Tri-Motor, Fokker F-10 and Sikorsky S-38 aeroplanes for their services.

90

Of the 21 "point-to-point" records Britain holds nine, and although not yet homologated, it seems certain that Henshaw's magnificent return trip will net him four of these – the London-Cape and Cape-London solo records, and the same records irrespective of personnel. All four of these records were formerly held by Britain, represented by Miss Amy Johnson, H. L. Brook and the Clouston-Kirby-Green equipage.

In the same category comes another remarkable flight, now four years old and still unsurpassed. In the Robertson Trophy race of 1934 Scott and Campbell Black put half the world behind them in just under three days – an average speed of nearly 160 m.p.h. Even the flight of the Clouston-Ricketts combination, which gained the four London-Sydney and London-Wellington and back records, falls short of this effort. The fastest of the later trips – four years after the race – was 29 m.p.h. slower than the Melbourne flight.

Probably one of the most note-worthy, but least publicized, trans-oceanic flights to rank as a record was the return Berlin-New York journey of the German Focke Fw. 20w in August last year. Henke and von Moreau, with a mechanic and radio operator, left Staaken on August 10th, and returned to Berlin on the 14th – averaging 158 m.p.h. out and 199 m.p.h. on the return trip from Floyd Bennett Field to Tempelhof.

Of the remaining long-distance awards, the United States holds four – London to New York, New York to Los Angeles and back, and Havana to Washington. Italy has one – Rome to Rio de Janeiro – and France four gained principally along the Paris-Cochin China route. The 94-hour Tokyo to London record of 1937 stands to Japan's credit.

In this field, at all events, we hold our own, but here the tale of our distinctions ends. Apart from the Vickers Wellesley formation flight we have no absolute records. The High Flight Section of the Italian Air Force holds the heavier-than-air altitude record – although in this particular ding-dong game its tenure is never very secure, and Pezzi's 56,100 feet will almost certainly be exceeded at least once this year. Japan's 7,235-mile closed-circuit flight still remains unbeaten although the Wellesley seems

Germany, 1934 - Hitler came to power in 1933, and ex-world War I ace Herman Goering, a member of the Reichstag who had supported aviation since 1929, was appointed Air Minister.

quite capable of surpassing it; and, of course the speed record seems depressingly safe with Italy. On the aerostation side, the U.S.A. "Explorer II's" 72,000 feet effort is scarcely likely to invite competition from this country.

Unfortunately, we don't go to gas-bags these days for our aeronautical exercises, otherwise there would probably be a few more records on our slate. The duration figure of 87 hours which Kaulen put up for Germany has been waiting to be attacked since 1913; and the 1,896-mile distance record – also Germany's – is 24 years old. But the record-holders have turned their attention to dirigible aerostation, and here they have no fear of competition. The only possible challenge which the "Graf Zeppelin's" ten-year-old Lakehurst to Freidrichshafen record is likely to evoke will come from L.Z.130.

German and Gliding

Thanks largely to Versailles, Germany has distinguished herself since the war as a country of gliding enthusiasts, who share with the U.S.S.R. all the major awards in motorless flight. The Russian Rastorgueff holds the distance record with a flight of 405 miles, whilst Germany still retains the 36 hours duration record set up in a Baby Grunau in 1933. Poland, a country usually associated with free ballooning, is the only nation that aspires to motor-glider records; she holds the only two that are recognized.

Helicopters

The five helicopter records are all monopolised by Germany's Focke Fw.61 VI – probably the most successful aircraft of its type evolved. This machine is being developed very rapidly, and performance figures are constantly going up. The last homologated flight duration record stands at one hour twenty minutes, and last year Ewald Rohlfs, who holds four out of the five records, averaged 122.5 kms.p.h. (about 76 m.p.h.) over a measured 20 kilometres.

To-day's record is to-morrow's routine – a comforting reflection for those who must needs search for something "useful" in second-splitting. That is a half-truth, of course. We look forward to utilising, not yesterday's record, but the ones set up twenty years ago. Consider the history of Atlantic flight; and remember that it takes over twice as long to get to the Cape to-day by airline as it took Scott and Black to get to Melbourne four years ago.

Handley Page study - in a period rich in eccentric characters and extraordinary tales, Sir Frederick Handley-Page stands out. Pioneer of the British aviation industry, he claimed his works to be the first to be constructed solely for the manufacture of aircraft.

HALF AN HOUR WITH HENSHAW
An interview with the Cape Record Breaker
1939

"Fog was beginning to roll up at Gravesend Airport when I took off at 3 o'clock in the morning. I didn't see the Channel; that and the whole of France was under fog, so I went over at 9,000 feet. The first piece of land I saw after leaving Gravesend was Africa – though I did see the lights of Paris glowing up through the fog at one point. Dawn broke when I was near Minorca, but I did not see the island, and when the clock showed that the Atlas Mountains were fifteen minutes ahead I nosed down through the stuff to find Oran. Severe icing conditions made me climb again and turn east for thirty miles. Then we got down without much trouble."

"But tell me, Mr. Henshaw, with no wireless and not seeing any landmark since leaving England, how could you possibly locate Oran?"

Fighting the Weather

"Well, if you have good instruments and trust them, a fast aeroplane like the Mew Gull does not get very far off its course even in a beam wind. I relied on the forecast, which said I should drift west at 25 m.p.h., and steered my course accordingly."

"But did you find that the weather forecasts were always accurate?"

"As a matter of fact, down the whole length of Africa and back again to Oran I did not have a weather forecast. I could not have afforded to delay even if they were unfavourable, and certainly down from Goa to Libreville, the forecasts would not have been favourable as I was caught during the night in an intense tropical storm and I got the biggest battering I have ever had. Since I could not climb over the storm I had to go through it and for five hours I saw nothing but my instruments. The air was so rough that I had to fight all the time to keep the machine the right way up, and after a thousand miles of this I felt so worn out that I didn't care what happened."

"And were you still on your course after flying blind through that weather?" "Yes. As, a matter of fact, I was and the surprise did much to revive me."

"Did you have any worse experience during the trip ?"

A Narrow Squeak

"Well, perhaps the take-off at Libreville gave me the biggest fright. The aerodrome there is a strip 1,900 yards long of shingle and sand. They are in the process of improving the surface and there is a deep ditch across the middle which limited the run available to 600 yards. In England this would have been sufficient even with a full load of petrol, but in the tropics the thin air means that you need all the run you can get. I had a very anxious time as the plane accelerated towards this ditch, and as it approached the wheels were still pattering on the ground at over 80 m.p.h.; and she didn't lift until the ditch seemed only a few feet away – but she just made it. That was the nearest squeal of the whole journey."

"I suppose after all this you must have been pretty nearly all-in when you got to Cape Town?"

"Yes, I was terribly tired, and sitting flat on the floor of the plane, my legs stuck straight out in front, giving me a sort of cramp in the stomach – the muscles would tighten up over my ribs, so much so that I had to push them down into place."

"How could you land a fast aeroplane as tired as you were then ?"

"I don't know – it seems that when an

This Flying Business - Glenn Curtiss is justly remembered as the leading pioneer of seaplanes. Curtiss and Wright had merged by 1930.

emergency arises there is always a little reserve of energy still left. But after the landing I was near to passing out. Besides the actual physical tiredness, another thing which gets you down is the sudden change in climate. I had been frozen nearly stiff passing over the Atlas Mountains, and within twelve hours I was sweating buckets as we crossed the Equator."

Fuel Problem

"The advantage of youth was on your side then, Mr. Henshaw. I should think an older man might have no reserves left for the final landing."

"Yes, I suppose youth does count and, as a matter of fact, so do physical jerks – do you know that, for about a month before the flight started, home was something like a boxer's training camp?"

"Bye the bye, Mr. Henshaw, there are two questions I've always wanted to ask a long-distance airman. The first is "How do you manage about food during the flight?" and the second is "How do you arrange for fuel for the plane at some of the out-of-the-way aerodromes?"

"Well, No.1 is easy enough to answer. I take a supply of fruit, two apples and oranges, and for drinking I have two thermos flasks strapped to a rack just behind my head, with rubber tubes attached. When I want a drink of either orange juice or milk I just suck the appropriate tube. The second is a little more difficult – plans for refuelling the plane have to be made long before the flight commences, in order that supplies may be available. But the firms concerned have now got quite used to seeing a pile of the familiar Castrol tins against a background of dusky mechanics."

The Return Journey

"What about the trip back? Did you have better weather?"

"Yes. On the whole it was easier weather, but fog was blanketing Mossamedes where I was due before dawn."

"What did you do then with your petrol running low?"

"I circled around waiting for a sea breeze to roll back the mist. In about ten minutes – it seemed like an hour – I saw four flares gleaming

through the fog. When approaching to land I wanted to open the window on my right for a clearer view, and that window nearly caused an accident. It is held shut by a hook and when I moved the hook it caught into my forefinger. I had already shut the throttle, so the machine was losing height rapidly and my left hand, being caught in this way, was obscuring my view and preventing me from opening up the engine again. It all happened in a few seconds and, as the ground came up towards me, I jerked my finger free just in time to smack the throttle open and go round the aerodrome again."

"Had there been an accident then, I don't suppose anyone would have guessed that it was due to the window catch. After Libreville your next stop was Gao. Had you any further difficulties there?"

"Yes. That was another difficult take off because there was no proper lighting for a take off at night – just four hurricane lamps set out in

THIS FLYING BUSINESS

"I suppose we shall soon travel by
air-vessels; make air instead of sea voyages;
and at length find our way to the moon,
in spite of the want of atmosphere"

Lord Byron (1882)

First Europe, and then the globe, will be linked by flight, and nations so knit together that they will grow to be next door neighbours. This conquest of the air will prove, ultimately, to be man's greatest and most glorious triumph. What railways have done for nations, airways will do for the world.

CLAUDE GRAHAME-WHITE & HARRY HARPER (1914)

It is impossible to over-estimate the importance of the ground staff; reliability, safety, and economy - three foundation stones on which the goodwill of aviation must be erected - depend on their efficiency. It is true to say that the man on the ground keeps the machine in the air.

ETHERTON

The interior of the airline terminal in Victoria, London, in the late 1930s - the original Imperial town terminal was a house in Mayfair.

Winged Cunarder - the sumptuously appointed forward cabin of an Imperial airliner of the "Heracles" class. Imperial remained loyal to the stately H.P.42 "Hannibal" and H.P.45 "Heracles".

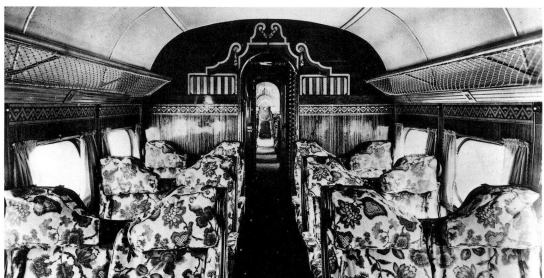

New York to Utah at 157 m.p.h.
by C. S. Staniland, 1935

Southampton (Hampshire) to Salt Lake City (Utah,U.S.A.). Wednesday, August 21st, *Speed of the Wind* departed in the *Majestic* from Southampton bound for New York, thence by rail out to the Bonneville Salt Beds, 130 miles west of Salt Lake City in the State of Utah, to make an attempt on the world's 24-hour record, accompanied by her three drivers, George Eyston, Albert Denly and myself, also her designer, the late Ernest Eldridge, and two mechanics, Len Ainsley and Tom Harvey.

As far as New York we had the pleasure of the company of Mrs. Eyston and two small Eystons; unfortunately, after the first day out not much was seen of the small Eystons owing to slight disturbances of the ever-doubtful Atlantic! Anyhow it was a very pleasant crossing, incidentally, my first. I won't waste time on that as no doubt it was the same as any other crossing.

We were joined at Cherbourg by W. F. Bradley, who was the team manager. He had no wrong ideas about training, though!

The day after getting into New York, which was August 27th, the car was on the train bound for the west.

After a brief look round New York, and several bad frights in taxis, we left by United Air Lines from Newark Field on August 29th. As we were a fairly large party, numbering seven, Reid Railton, the designer of Sir Malcolm Campbell's car, having joined us, we had a Boeing 247D all to ourselves for the journey. Incidentally, Sir Malcolm was about one hour ahead of us, also on his way to the Salt Beds where he subsequently put the world's mile and kilometre records up to over 300 m.p.h.

First, a word about the Boeing 247D. These machines are used exclusively by United Air Lines, who are one of the biggest air lines in the States, and are also used by other lines as well.

They carry ten passengers, two pilots and an air hostess. A twin engine machine, two Pratt and Whitney Wasps, giving all told about 1,100h.p. An all-metal machine which cruises at 8,000 ft. at 175 m.p.h.

Salt Lake City is about 2,057 miles from New York and we were there 13 hours after starting, which meant an average of just 157 m.p.h., including stops! These figures speak for themselves; further, these machines are now nearly out of date and they hope shortly to be replacing them with new machines with a cruising speed very much in excess of this! Good luck to them; they deserve it.

As in the air, so on the ground, no time is wasted; your luggage is weighed, you are handed a check for it, shown into the machine, and off it goes. It's taxied out to the end of the run-way when the pilot runs up both engines on the brakes. Then straight off, turn on to the course, pull up the wheels, and climb up to 8,000 ft. at an air speed of 130 m.p.h. At 8,000 ft, which is the most efficient height of the machine, it's levelled out, the airscrews are changed to the course pitch, and the machine is settled down to a cruising speed of about 175 m.p.h.

Fortunately, through various friends, such as Lester Gardner, and introductions, I was allowed to fly the machines as much as I wanted and allowed to study the organisation from the pilot's point of view.

Before going any further, I should like to say how very much we all appreciated the way in which we were treated by the pilots and air hostesses all along the line; in fact, all the time we were travelling by air. Nothing was too much trouble for them, they never seemed tired of explaining their machines, organisation, or anything to do with the flight.

Seaplane development progressed between the two World Wars and the four-engine Sikorsky S-40 was one of the largest. It was replaced in 1934 by the S-42.

99

A panorama of Rio harbour appears on this passenger tariff for Syndicato Condor. The Condor tri-motored floatplanes were variations of the standard German transport, the legendary Junkers 52/3M.

I think their companies must treat them fairly well and don't overwork them. On this run, the usual times seemed to be, first pilot would go about 2½ – 3½ hours, second pilot and stewardess about 4 – 5 hours. Illustrated below is a rough schedule of the stopping places, times and changes.

> 1 New York to Cleveland 405 miles –
>   2½ hours.
> 2. First pilot changed.
> 3. Second pilot and stewardess on to
>   Chicago 319 miles – 2 hours.
> 4. At Chicago, first pilot changed, also
>   second pilot and stewardess.
> 5. Chicago to Omaha 426 miles – 2.40 hours.
> 6. First pilot changed.
> 7. Omaha to Cheyenne 482 miles –
>   2.40 hours.
> 8. Second pilot and stewardess changed.
> 9. Cheyenne to Salt Lake City 415 miles –
>   2 hours.

It should be noted that the west bound journey nearly always encounters head winds, and that the eastbound journeys are made at a very much higher average speed, in the region of 170 m.p.h. or more.

These Boeings are most pleasant and are certainly not tiring to fly, although I was fairly tired when we got to Salt Lake City – this was only owing to the extreme hospitality of the pilots, who allowed, or in fact, insisted on my flying the machine – I must have flown it for about 9 hours! I don't think each pilot as he came on realised that I had been flying it most of the way! Anyhow, it was a great experience which I wouldn't have missed for anything.

These machines are very stable and have no vices; although they have no flaps, they touch down at only about 60 m.p.h. and can be pulled up with their very efficient brakes in a short distance – they have to be, as some of their aerodromes aren't too large!

Although I am not a blind flying pilot, we encountered quite a severe snow storm between Chicago and Omaha in which I flew blind for about an hour. With the aid of their instruments, which must be pretty well perfect, I had no trouble at all except for George Eyston, who occasionally put his head round the door and said "Where are all the other machines?" Actually, there is no danger of collisions, as the ground officials tell you at what height and just where another machine is that may be near you. Each machine has to send out its position, height, speed, various temperature readings, and what weather conditions it's flying in, every half hour. In turn the ground send out weather reports from the various stations which may concern you, at half hourly intervals.

The next thing is finding the way. Nothing could be easier. They work on the wireless beam. You hear, if you are on your course, a long continuous buzz, the letter "T" in the Morse code, which is punctuated every few seconds by the call sign, which is another letter, of the

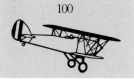

The romance and excitement of air cruising, 1936 - "Clipper" had become a Pan American trademark. An artist's impression of the cabin of a Sikorsky S-42.

station you are making for, or leaving. Should you be off your course you will hear an underlying letter "A" which means you are to the South, or an "N" which means to the North.

These two letters switch about, according to which zone you are flying in, but this is all clearly marked on a chart in the pilot's compartment. Anyhow, there is no chance of any muddling, as the pilots always stick to the same routes.

At night, all the routes are lighted by revolving red and white beacons, about 10 miles apart, and every 30 miles or so there is an emergency landing ground which is denoted by a revolving green and white beacon.

This organisation applies to every main air route all over the United States.

No time is wasted in coming down. When within about twenty miles of the aerodrome, if the type of country permits, the nose is put slightly down. This is for two reasons: one being the shortest way in time of coming down, the other in order not to put too much stress on the passengers' ears.

When within three or four miles of the aerodrome, the pilot lets the ground know he is ready to come in. If they are ready and the aerodrome is clear, they say so. Something of this sort goes on.

Pilot – "Am four miles east of field and ready to come in."

Ground – "O.K. Eddie, field's clear, get your wheels down, wind west about 10 miles an

hour, one ship circling towards you north-east of field, watch it. All right you're clear, in you come."

Once on the ground no time is lost in slow taxi-ing, the machine being taxied quickly and right up to the airport main building where the ground staff is ready waiting to unload, or load luggage, and fill up with fuel. The stops last from twelve to fifteen minutes, sometimes shorter than that if it's only a matter of changing machines, as if this is necessary the other machine is waiting all ready.

The last section of the run from Cheyenne (incidentally, this is pronounced "shyan." When we heard them talking we thought they said "Siam" which seemed rather unnecessarily far off the course!) was done at night.

We took off from Cheyenne at dusk; the aerodrome there is 6,000 ft. above sea level and in the westward distance could be seen the mountains rising up in great black masses to 12,000 ft. It was most impressive sitting in front of that Boeing watching them get closer. We actually only went up to 11,000 ft., as in good weather they fly through the passes following the beacons.

This country from Wyoming into Utah looks very uninviting, there being few places for forced landings, and practically completely uninhabited. After dark there are hardly any lights to be seen, except the revolving beacons, and every so often the outlining lights of an emergency landing ground, which is a very comforting sight.

Airline schedules from 1933. The gigantic German seaplane, the Dornier Wal, was used by Condor, the South American agent for the *Graf Zeppelin*.

On a really dark night, such as the one we struck, it's nearly as good as blind flying, as there is no horizon, everything being jet black in front. I found it much easier to fly on the instruments instead of straining to try to see out.

The most impressive sight of the whole journey was the arrival at Salt Lake City which is 4,000 ft. above sea level, and lies right under the mountains on its east side with the desert stretching away to its west.

Just before getting to the city the mountains go up to 12,000 ft. and the beacon route lies down the valley, which is a steep one with mountains up to 12,000 ft. on the left and 10,000 ft. on the right. We flew down this valley losing height all the time with the black masses rising steeply up on each side and suddenly, round the edge of one of the mountains, we came out over Salt Lake City 4,000 ft. below us, and when I say it is one of the most beautiful cities in the world and lacks nothing in lighting effects, it can well be imagined what a magnificent sight it was.

The same procedure for coming in at night was adopted as in daylight. They land entirely on the aerodrome outline lights and the two searchlights carried just outboard of each engine.

So the end of a most pleasant and interesting journey. Practically across the Continent in 13 hours and no stunt at that, just an ordinary journey as carried out daily without any fuss.

There was no lack of food during the journey either, in fact, they just kept on giving us a meal called lunch, and a very good lunch, or good lunches rather, they were. After about our second lunch within three hours, a new air hostess got on at Chicago and soon after leaving, started to deal out yet another lunch. She put the tray down in front of Reid Railton who said, "No, thank you, I've already had lunch." whereupon she answered "Don't be a cissy, have another!"

Anything you may hear against the American air lines, don't believe it – they are just about one hundred per cent.

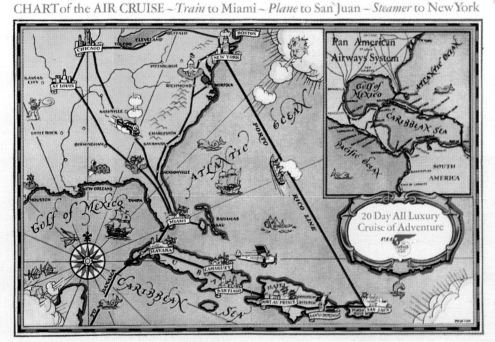

CHART of the AIR CRUISE ~ *Train* to Miami ~ *Plane* to San Juan ~ *Steamer* to New York

De Luxe travel is offered by train, plane and steamer in 1929, when several rail-air itineraries were introduced. The need for the rail links had all but disappeared by the end of 1930.

103

IT'S QUICKER BY AIR
by Flt. Lt. "Tommy Rose" 1937

In these highly competitive days, speed is the essence of business. Speed and safety in travel are all-important factors. That is why this is an age of air travel. SPEED is the life blood of air transport. If it wasn't for the fact that aircraft are considerably faster than land or sea transport it is possible that air transport wouldn't exist at all.

It costs more. It presents many more problems to the line operator. Very large sums have to be laid down before the hope of a profit can appear, and, not by any means least, a large amount of public inertia has to be conquered before the average traveller can be induced to fly at all. That they do fly – and in ever increasing numbers proves the value of speed.

But even that big word speed has to be split up into several headings by the harassed airline operator. What is fast on one airline is slow on another. What was very fast a year or so ago is now regarded as slower than the snail.

To make matters worse, the average traveller steps in again. By now he has absorbed enough air knowledge to be able to put forward a good deal of criticism. Not much of it is constructive. He reads about airlines in the U.S.A. travelling at average speeds of 185 to 190 m.p.h. He picks up on his travels statistics about European airlines. And he wants to know why his own airlines don't travel faster. He doesn't take into his argument at all the various problems that his own particular airline operator has to face,

Take an example. Airline travel is certainly fast at 100 miles an hour. But a machine that travels over the same route at 200 miles an hour is of more value to the traveller than the slower rival. He travels by air because he wants to get there quickly.

Therefore the 200 m.p.h. line should take all the traffic. But it isn't as simple as that. Suppose the high-speed line had a higher accident list, then the average traveller, by majority, would travel by the slow line.

Suppose again, that the 200 m.p.h. time was very uncomfortable compared to the 100 m.p.h. line. Once more our average traveller would go by the slow line.

But if the two lines offered equal safety and

Extreme luxury - stewards in starched jackets, served a piping-hot four course meal for fortunate Imperial travellers. The Captain, if tasks allowed, would join the passengers at lunch, which was presented on the blue and white company china. Napery, sterling silver cutlery, silver cruet and crystal wine glasses were laid on every table.

equal comfort – or nearly equal comfort – the fast line would win every time. This, to the traveller, sounds very simple. Why don't they do it? he asks.

One of the reasons is that it is very difficult to design and produce a high speed, comfortable airliner that will work at its high speed on a cost rate that produces profits. And it isn't much fun for the airline operator if he's got to run all his machines at a loss to himself. The line wouldn't last very long.

In the old days no commercial aircraft were comfortable. The travellers, mostly big business men, sacrificed a great deal for the sake of the speed that the aeroplane could offer them.

Things have changed since then. Nowadays, every new commercial aircraft that is produced has a great degree of comfort – in some instances comparable to a Pullman train, and in other instances better than that.

Speeds on these comfortable new aircraft increase with the comfort. Passengers can find

This publicity shot from Imperial Airways was probably posed for the cameras. Earplugs were offered to every passenger as the noise level could be deafening.

INTERIOR SALOON.

The saloon interior, complete with wicker seating, captures the spirit of its time. Woods and fabric were often the best to be found. Call buttons, lavatories, folding tables, galleys and reading lights had all made their appearance by the mid-1930s.

A Swedish Air Lines poster - Legagneux, on a Voisin, made the first flight in Sweden at Stockholm in July, 1909.

little to complain about. They can, and do, find a great deal to complain about on some operating schedules. But even those are being speeded up, slowly but surely.

So the passenger himself, who likes his speed and likes his comfort, is being well looked after.

But what about those hundreds of thousands of inanimate passengers that are carried everyday on every service of every major international airline?

I'm talking about the airmails. Those little white packets aren't being looked after as well as they might be. Take the present system. You post a letter to South Africa. The little fellow goes into the blue pillar box, or into the Post Office. He goes through the usual registration and then he's put in a van which takes him to Croydon Airport.

At Croydon Airport he's put into a bag with thousands of his fellows, and piled into the mail compartment of the Imperial Airways liner which is due for the first leg of the South Africa service.

He follows the fortunes of the living passengers in that machine all the way. He arrives at Cape Town about a week after he leaves Croydon. Soon they'll cut that time down to four days, or they intend to.

But that little white envelope doesn't want the comfort and the cossetting that his living companions do. All it wants is to get to its destination as soon as possible.

That isn't an impossible request. There are aircraft nowadays quite capable of reaching the Cape in two days perhaps less. They can carry a fairly large load of freight. But they can't offer the Pullman car comfort of their bigger and slower brothers. And it isn't so difficult to design a small, economical, high-speed craft as it is to design a big one. Why not send the mails round the Empire and round the world on these smaller and faster machines? Important though it is to the big machines, speed is the absolute life of air transport for the air mails. Those letters go by air because they are urgent, because they are first-class mail. They deserve to get to their destinations as quickly as it is humanly possible to send them.

That's where I think the real need lies. Give us speed by all means. It's essential. But segre-

AEROTRANSPORT
SWEDISH AIR LINES

gate your speed. Provide speed plus comfort for the passenger and speed plus speed for the international mails.

Send the passengers by the big, comfortable ships. Send the mails by the smaller, faster, but equally reliable mail-planes. It's not a new idea, after all. It is done on some American lines. The French and Germans use the system over the South Atlantic ocean. If you have a passenger machine with a 200 miles an hour maximum you can get a smaller mail machine with a 250 or more m.p.h. maximum.

Then, I think, everyone would be happy. The high speed which the airlines can and do give would be utilised down to the last possible mile.

And it's my opinion that the costs would be no higher, while the profits would rise. It is, after all, a proven fact that people will pay for speed. You can sell speed easier than anything else.

Why not sell it as much as possible? It's an attractive proposition.

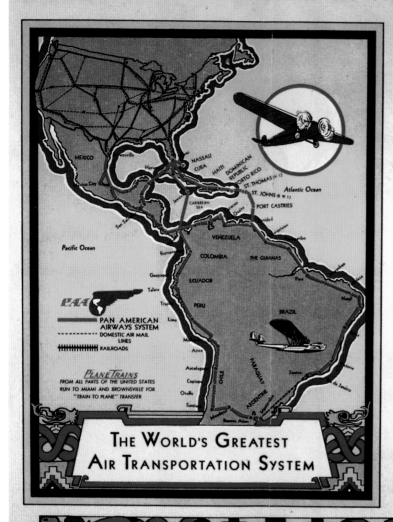

A Pan American brochure from the formative period of US air transport. Pan American became prominent in the use of flying boats and their North Atlantic service broke new ground.

Off for Paris - drawn for *The Sphere* magazine by W. Bryce Hamilton. For those who preferred to shop in the Rue de la Paix, the start of an Imperial airliner from its home base Croydon. Le Bourget airport in Paris was a place of unimaginable excitement and glamour (it was from here that many of the great pioneering services to Africa and the Orient had departed).

TO LINK THE EMPIRE
1937

The latest triumph of British aeronautical engineers, heralding the start of a new era in British civil aviation. Such are the well-founded claims of Imperial Airways, in connection with the new fleet of Empire Flying Boats which are now rapidly going into service.

These new flying boats embody many major improvements and modifications, and are equipped with every latest, well-tested flying and navigational device. It is the opinion of experts that they will prove superior to any other type of marine aircraft in the world.

An innovation in these aircraft is that they are of the unbraced, high-wing monoplane type with wing-tip floats. All previous marine aircraft on the Empire routes have been a product of biplane construction.

They have a span of 114 feet, an overall length of 882 feet, and the total loaded weight is approximately 18 tons, of which five tons will be available for passengers, mail, and freight, on a normal stage flight.

The aircraft are each powered with four Bristol "Pegasus" engines, which develop a total of approximately 4,000 h.p., and an indication of future service speeds is that *Canopus* did over 199 m.p.h. on official trials. The "Pegasus"

engine, incidentally, is similar in type to that fitted in the altitude record aeroplane.

The Empire flying-boats have two decks, the first time in aircraft construction that such a design has been utilised. Twenty-four passengers can be carried with every great comfort and convenience.

The capabilities of this type were indicated recently, when, on Tuesday January 12th, one of the new fleet – the *Centaurus* – left Alexandria on an experimental long distance flight. Carrying eight passengers in addition to its crew, and one ton of mail, the *Centaurus* reached Brindisi (1,000 miles) on Tuesday afternoon. It left Brindisi at 5.30p m, bound for Marseilles, a distance of 850 miles, which it covered in 4 hours 57 mins., at an average speed of approximately 172 m.p.h. Leaving Marseilles at 11.15 on Wednesday morning, it made a long detour over France, completing 650 miles on arrival at Southampton at 4.15. Its total flying time for the whole journey was about 16 hours and the distance covered nearly 2,500 miles, an average speed under normal service conditions of over 150 m.p.h.

An enormous amount of preparation has been necessary for the introduction of the new services, on which the route covered will eventually be to and from England, Africa, India, the Far East, the Straits Settlements and Australia.

The British Short flying boat "Caribou". Short flying boats offered commodious and comfortable service in an effort to rival the traditional luxury of travel at sea.

An interesting feature necessitated by these preparations is a fleet of 60 high speed sea going motor craft equipped to act as floating control stations, being built to service the Empire flying boats. This fleet is of great interest to speed enthusiasts, being constructed by the designers and builders of the famous Miss England and Miss Britain series of motor boats. Each craft will be powered with twin 100h.p. engines capable of accelerating, with a full load of two tons, to 28 m.p.h. from rest in under eight seconds.

The introduction of the new Empire flying boats is in connection with the Government's scheme for the development of the Empire air routes, which, briefly, covers a very material improvement on present schedule between the

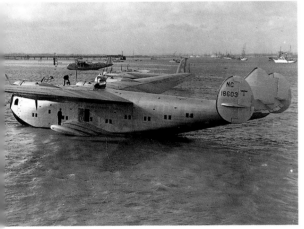

different parts of the Empire; a substantial increase in the frequency of the services; and revision of postal charges, whereby all first-class mail will be carried by air throughout the Empire without surcharge thus enabling letters to be despatched to India, Australia, Africa and the Far East for 1½d. up to half-an ounce, a sweeping development in postal arrangements almost on a par with the introduction of the penny post.

The existing Empire air mail schedules will be speeded up as more and more of the new aircraft are commissioned and as ground or-ganisation for night operations is perfected along the routes. When the scheme is complete, the air journey from England to India will be reduced from the present six days to only a little over two days.

Singapore or Cape Town will be a four days' journey as against eight and a half days at present, and the flight to Australia, which takes twelve and a half days by present time tables, will be completed in just over a week.

The new aircraft will be known as the "C" class flying boats, and will all be given names which commence with that initial letter.

The air mail scheme will be put into opera-tion on the African route in May. It will be extended to India a few months later, when yet further extensions will be made to include the Far East and the Straits Settlements.

A colourful promo-tion for the "Planetrain". Charles Lindbergh's successful solo flight across the North Atlantic in 1927 had awakened the Americans to the possibilities and prospects of air travel.

Yankee Clipper **arrives at South-ampton watched by a crowd on the Clashot. She is being moored after completion of her trans-Atlantic survey flight, with 21 passengers on board.**

111

Pan American selected the Fokker F-10 Tri-Motor for these 1929 schedules. The credentials of Dutchman Anthony Fokker were further confirmed when his aircraft were chosen by such greats as aviators and air explorers Admiral Byrd, Amelia Earhart and Charles Kinsford-Smith.

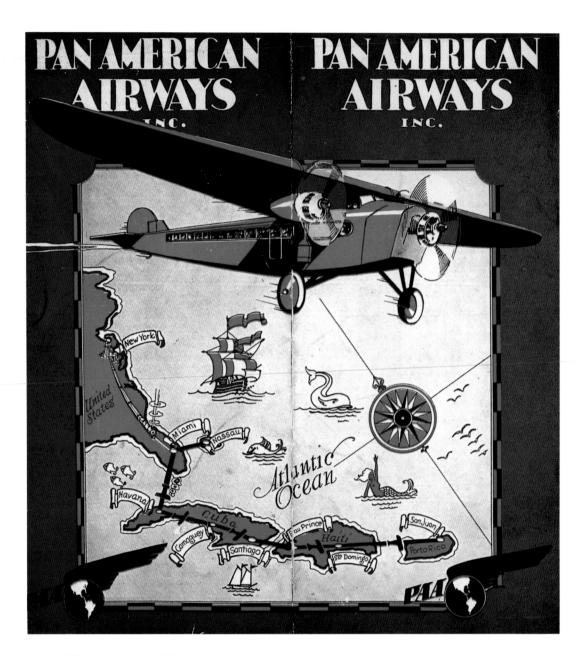

WINGS ACROSS THE ATLANTIC
By Leslie E. Wells, 1937

This summer will see the dawn of a new era in world transport, with the introduction of the first regular trans-Atlantic air service.

Has the influence of flying bestowed a sanctimonious effect on humanity, or a curse? Sea communications to remote parts of the world built up the British Empire: will air travel protect them? In the years to follow, will the services of the air determine the performance in the uniformity of the Empire: Consider these record flights

– Australia in less than six days from England; Cape Town, South Africa, within four days; India in three days; Persia and Egypt only eighteen hours from time of leaving London – these are achievements by air in reach of today. What will tomorrow bring we ask? We leave that to the powers of darkness! But, where does Britain stand?

A New Era

Well, this summer will see the beginning of yet another new era in aviation, the prospect of a trans-Atlantic air service, via London, Ireland,

across the Atlantic to Harbour Grace, Newfoundland, on to Montreal and New York.

In the meantime, while this war is about to begin for the skyways across the Atlantic, there are many forecasts regarding the future of air travel which seem to possess an impression of Jules Verne about them. But young men who have grown up with this comparatively new industry frequently totter to make predictions, so swift has been the progress and so amazing some of its exploitations. As on land and sea, the air is the speed god of swift travel which has brought about wonders.

The present air speed record is 440 miles per hour set up by Francisco Appelo; on water, 125 miles per hour by Gar Wood, on land, 301 miles per hour by Sir Malcolm Campbell. And they are speeds within the limits of safety.

In the world to-day airplanes still continue to grow larger and faster, while the earth below appears to grow smaller. Flights in airplanes on record-breaking non-stop journeys prove that slowly the stretches of distance are being conquered, from eleven miles to 5,900 miles in twenty-eight years. So we may gather from this that distance is being drastically reduced.

Round the World in 14 Days!

On the map, in place of out-of-date trade routes, new ones spring up. Air traffic bases in far-away places like Australia, native islands of Africa, and rocky islands in the Pacific have been re-built into modern airports, incorporating all the latest meteorological instruments, lighting systems, and everything for up-to-the-minute air bases.

In less than five years people in Britain may be able to obtain a ticket for a complete all-round-the-world flight in less than fourteen days, including stops for restocking with food, overhauling, refuelling, and other minor requirements, etc.

Lonely Air Routes

Not only is air transport a boon to fast travelling, but it reaches most unexpected places inland, and across the loneliest wastes of the widest ocean. Therefore, it will be no surprise if, to-morrow, backwoodsmen find themselves on or

adjacent to a busy air traffic lane; or if the equivalent of floating lighthouses, equipped as radio meteorological and rescue aids to the third-dimension navigator, are maintained in mid-ocean.

Already, British airplane companies are busy on the building of a number of luxury air liners for the proposed trans-Atlantic commercial flight scheme. Beginning about October 15th, flights will be made from London, via Spain, the Azores, and Bermuda. At all times the weather conditions will govern the choice of the first landing station.

The end of last year saw the close of many years' study of oceanic commercial flight possibilities. The conferences held at Ottawa and Washington in December, 1935, brought closer to actuality the prospect, so long heralded, of a trans-Atlantic air service for passengers and mail. In effect, agreement was sought, and reached, between the British Empire and the United States for a joint service across the North Atlantic; and a base in the estuary of the Shannon has been chosen as its European junction.

Air progress - aviation reached South America and Asia in 1910. The first flights took place in the Argentine and Brazil and, in Indo-China, from Saigon.

113

Always over the water - Pacific Marine Airways was bought by Western Express in 1928; Wilmington-Catalina Airlines operated the route from 1931.

TAC started an over-the-water service in 1929 and had changed their name to Transamerican Airlines Corporation by 1931. Note the use of "speed" lines by the artist on the Keystone-Loening Air Yacht.

114

The Composite 'Plane

Britain's offer for the first trans-Atlantic air mail will depend experimentally on an invention of Major R.H. Mayo, known as the composite aircraft. This type of 'plane is designed to obviate some of the difficulties of long range fast flight; actually, the composite plan was patented in Germany by Professor Hugo Junkers twenty or more years ago. The belief is held that a comparatively small range machine can be helped by a "porter" 'plane, after which it would proceed for the next 1,000 miles or so.

The composite aircraft combines a heavy, long-range, four-engined mono-plane that is attached on top of the flying-boat in taking off, to form an eight-engined biplane. When the crafts are in the air and at full speed, the lifting monoplane cuts off and returns to the aerodrome, while the big ship continues on its journey with a pay load which would have been too heavy for it alone to lift of the ground. A considerable part of the load carried must be consumable or dischargeable. In any long-range 'plane the load must consist largely of fuel and oil, and this load must necessarily be consumed by the end of the journey. The load of a military 'plane may be discharged in the form of bombs. As the two components are securely locked together, the composite craft can take off as a single unit from land in winter. But the safe landing, as well as the safe launching of such a machine, must be assured.

The cost of building radio guides for the route, which is expected to have newly designed beacons to be anchored near mid-ocean, is understood to be equally shared by both Governments.

While the complicated details are thus being thought out, let us consider the route to be taken by these luxury flying hotels.

About twice the distance by air from New-foundland to Ireland, the Bermuda-Azores route is, at present, the most likely route to be adopted, rather than the direct crossing, long recognized by experts as a passage attainable within the economic flight range of powerful 'planes operating within their normal range distance. On the other hand, the saving of time on the direct route from Newfoundland to Ireland or the Lizard, would, were it practicable within safety limits, represent an extremely valuable asset to the air transport company attempting to maintain a regular service along its billowy surface and storm-swept skies. By either way, London and New York would be less than thirty hours apart. By the southern route, via Bermuda or the Azores, London and Montreal would still be separated by a considerable flying distance in point of time.

The situation, therefore, is beset with the alternative of small pay loads lying in storm tracks from Newfoundland to Ireland, or detouring in mid-ocean to refuel at the Azores and Bermuda. While to some extent the American viewpoint favours small pay loads, the view of the British and French is definitely in favour of large pay loads and low rates in short hops utilizing to the fullest extent the islands of Bermuda as the Atlantic's western aviation terminal. A fundamental reason for the difference in the European and the American points of view is that, unlike their American cousins, European fliers, crossing the Atlantic westward, have to fly against head winds and the west-to-east weather drift all the way.

A Short Empire flying boat, the *Golden Hind*. **Built by shipwrights at Rochester, Kent and powered by four supercharged 740 h.p. Bristol Pegasus engines, they were equally at home in two elements.**

A Curtiss Ford Tri-Motor loading passengers at Havana. By 1930, US airlines could be said to fall into two categories: those that operated the famous Tri-Motor and those that did not.

The Basic Question

The basic question is not the conceded practicability of the southern route as a safety detour, but whether the Great Circle course – blazed by Sir John Alcock and Sir Arthur Whitten Brown, Lindbergh, the rigid airship *R.34*, Sir Charles Kingsford-Smith, Dr. Hugo Eckener, and others – can be flown consistently on commercial non-stop schedule all the year round. So long as engines requiring hydrocarbon fuels are used to sustain and propel airplanes, the fuel load which must be carried for a flight distance of 3,000 miles will be substantially six times greater than that required for a flight of 500 miles.

Further, on any commercial basis, the dispatch of airplanes across the roof of the world, over sub-Arctic and Arctic Canada, Greenland, Iceland, the Faroe Islands, and Northern Ireland, is scarcely practicable at the moment. To the hazard of ice formation on the wings, there is added the peril of sporadic violent winds and of blind flying in fog.

On the American side, "China Clipper" flying boats, as used by Pan-American Airways on the Pacific Ocean, will be brought to start the trans-Atlantic service. It is actually one of the Glenn Martin 130 flying boats designed specially for trans-oceanic service to the order of Pan-American Airways. They are being used on the 8,200-mile service from San Francisco to Manila, Philippine Islands, the entire route being over the Pacific. Their actual flight range non-stop is 4,000 miles.

The Glenn Martin 130 is an all-metal flying boat with accommodation for forty-eight passengers, and is fitted with four 800 hp. Pratt and Whitney "Twin-Wasp" engines, which give it a cruising speed of 150 m.p.h. It weighs, fully loaded, 51,000 lbs.

Fokker's, the Dutch airplane manufacturers, have also commenced intense research work with a view to producing 'planes suitable for the institution of a regular trans-Atlantic service. In order to ensure commercial exploitability, these 'planes are designed so as to permit the transport of a large number of passengers.

Designs under consideration will permit the construction of giant five-engined 'planes, which are able to fly the New York to Amsterdam distance in 16 hours, carrying 36 passengers seated, or 18 passengers in berths. In spite of this extraordinary load, only a crew of five will be necessary to manage the flight. However, they do not intend to disclose further details until the first machine has been built and tested.

So much for the types of aircraft to be used. But, if these machines are to meet the broad essentials of speed with safety, regularity of service, economy in time and comfort, the Atlantic service must be shown to be reasonably safe, continuous and therefore commercially feasible. Can such a showing be made now with the best types of commercial aircraft? In storm and sunshine, throughout the year, can such claims be sustained on the Newfoundland to Ireland route ?

If not, there is at hand the seadrome, or floating steel and iron island airport, which some two years ago was approved as a Federal project of the United States Government. Although held in abeyance, the seadrome idea, ingenious if costly, has never been completely abandoned and it may be revived. Ocean flying accidents will, undoubtedly, reawaken official interest in the issue. In its favour, cost of construction has been reduced, models have been tested satisfactorily, and the structural design strengthened and simplified.

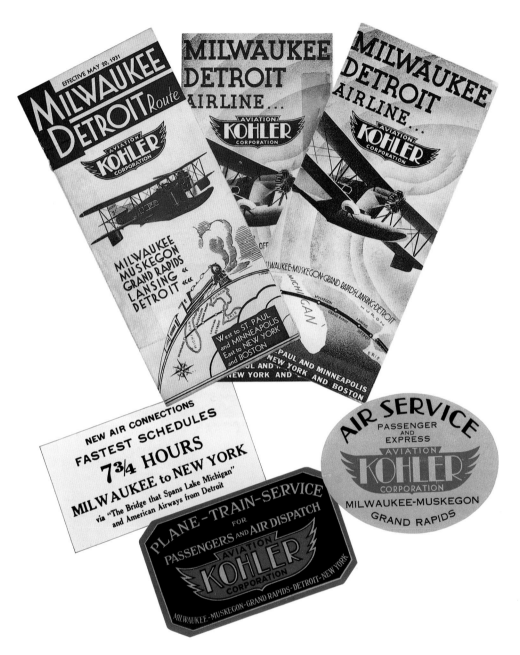

Baggage labels from Kohler Aviation, 1929 - 1934. The first international passenger air service (as opposed to mail) operated by a US airline was inaugurated in 1928 by Pan American from Key West in Florida.

What is a Seadrome?

The seadrome or mobile marine airplane dock consists of a steel and iron open-work truss structure with a six-acre deck, 100 feet above the water-line, supported by thirty-two buoyancy tanks or hollow steel supporting tubes, forty feet below water. Ballast chambers extend 208 feet below the surface; each buoyancy tank is about thirty-five feet in diameter, thus giving stability. The 'drome will be moored to a huge buoy, some 800 feet removed, which in turn will be attached by two 23,000-foot strands of steel cable to a 1,500-ton anchor lying on the ocean, bed. Around this buoy the seadrome will have at all times free and easy play for about one mile from it.

To meet any emergency, each sea-hangar will be equipped with 2,400 horse-power. At the rear, between sea and deck, will be stabilizers similar to those on the tails of airplanes and dirigibles. The net result will be motionless stability. The total displacement of the seadrome on service duty will be in excess of 65,000 tons, approximately one-third being ballast. Floodlights and boundary lights, similar to those at any land airport, will provide for night landings; and improved blind-flying equipment will guide pilots down to safe landings in fog.

Left:

The years of growth - Imperial Airways advertising with (from top to bottom): the "Heracles" and "Hannibal" class biplanes; *Scylla; Atalanta;* and *Scipio.*

Right:

The control tower at Croydon, on the outskirts of London, around 1934. Croydon, established as a military airfield during World War I, became the Customs airport for London, in succession to Hounslow, in 1920. The grand - for its time - terminal building, with domed booking hall, was constructed in 1928 and is still extant. One could watch aeroplanes taking off and landing from the flat roof of the Aerodrome Hotel, nearby, which survives today.

Mid-Atlantic Havens!

The plan is as novel and revolutionary as it is ingenious. A sea hangar, with six acres of unobstructed surface landing deck, three additional sub-decks, hotel accommodation for passengers who want to break their trip, meteorological and radio stations! Steel and cement floating islands across the ocean to serve as landing stations for airplanes carrying a heavier paying load than is now possible.

The top deck, from which airplanes will take off and on which they may alight, will be 1,500 feet long, 300 feet wide in the centre, tapering to 150 feet in width at bow and stern. It will be unobstructed, and airplanes that use it will be housed on a lower deck, to and from which they will be conveyed by an elevator. Each iron buoyancy tank divides into twelve water-tight compartments containing compressed air. Some of them will be used for water ballast and fuel storage for both 'planes and the sea-drome power plant. In case of leakage, each compartment will be capable of isolation from the others. Moreover, underwater storage tanks for petrol reduce the fire hazard.

Sooner or later Britain will have to take part in the servicing of a North Atlantic air route. In addition to furnishing personnel and supplies, such servicing – which is fundamentally more important for ocean crossing than for the average routes over land – will include the provision of new and illuminated aerodromes, radio equipment, meteorological instruments, and beacons to mark the routes at sea.

Then eventually – over the Atlantic as over the Pacific – the airplane pilot will be supplied with radio direction-finding signals and weather reports from land and ship, enabling him to pick his altitude with regard to wind, strength and direction, fog and temperature. Continuing development of the scientific technique involved brings nearer the day when all oceans will be spanned by the speed gods of the air riding on the silvery surface of the clouds.

SPEED ON THE EMPIRE AIR ROUTES
by William Courtenay, 1937

Would you care to fly at 200 m.p.h. as an ordinary passenger on the Empire air routes to South Africa or Australia, and would you like to find yourself travelling at the rate of 4,000 miles per day?

You might think this a mere vision. But it is not. It is a goal towards which we are steadily drawing near.

Three years ago, in October, 1934, C.W.A. Scott and the late Tom Campbell Black flew at 200 m.p.h. or more in their D.H. Comet racing monoplane from Mildenhall (Suffolk) to Melbourne, Australia. The world gasped, Yet the racing speeds of yesterday are the air liner time-tables of to-morrow.

They covered 2,500 miles in a non-stop "hop" of about 12 hours to Baghdad, and in similar giant strides from Iraq to Allahabad, India, Singapore and Darwin; they reached Australia in a little over two days and Melbourne in just under three days.

It is true they flew at breathless speed had no time to sleep or shave, stopped only to re-fuel, and ate practically nothing en-route.

It is also true that their twin-engine mono-plane was a flying petrol tank with no room for more than about 200 lbs. of load except their two selves. These, of course, are not the conditions in which the general air passenger will reach Melbourne from London in three days.

But three years have elapsed since we were given this example of what high speed could accomplish. Since then designers have wrested the secrets of high speed. Engines which were then of not more than about 500 to 600 h.p. are now available at nearly 1,000 h.p. The engines of 1,500 h.p. are now being tested. By 1940 the 2,000 h.p. engine – which is already far beyond the mere design stage – will be available for the air liner.

Since 1934 also we have said goodbye to the biplane, and the designers have concentrated on the swift monoplane of sleek streamline appearance and clean design. Even the flying boat has become a monoplane of the same racer lines as the Comet. Hence we find that Short Bros. have been able to design and build the Empire type of flying boat which can not only fly at 200 m.p.h., but which can take up to 24 passengers and fuel for about 800 miles and a big load of baggage freight and mail as well. These boats, of which 28 will this year be operating on the Empire routes, each have four engines and each engine develops 920 h.p. at the take-off.

Long haul Empire routes - the Armstrong-Whitworth Atalanta of 1932, which was the first four-engined transport monoplane to see regular service as a British airliner. It carried 20 passengers and cruised at 125 mph, but was outclassed by contemporary rivals from Holland, Germany and the US.

119

Fast and robust - the Short Sunderland Mark I, arguably the best defensively armed British military aircraft in service at the start of World War II.

But there is a difference between an aircraft which can fly at 200 m.p.h. and one which can guarantee to take air passengers all over the Empire routes at that speed.

Firstly, of course, no aircraft is flown "full out" at its top speed. This is too great a strain on the working parts of the engines. Besides, it puts up fuel consumption alarmingly. Consequently, the air liners are cruised at about 55 per cent. of their full throttle power, and the cruising speed of the 200 m.p.h. flying boat drops to 165 m.p.h. But while the boats can amble along nicely with full load at this speed between stages of a commercial air route, this is not the average speed at which the traveller flies. Head winds have to be taken into account and when the air liner is taxying, ascending and descending, more time is taken up at slow speeds. These still further reduce cruising speed on an overall journey. For instance, air liners capable of 200 m.p.h. top speed are only averaging 137 m.p.h. on air routes where the distance is 1,000 miles with four or five stops.

M.P.H. Guaranteed

The goal of air travel at 200 m.p.h. can only be reached, therefore, when the aircraft manufacturer provides aeroplanes capable of top speeds in excess of 200 m.p.h. For then the margin over 200 enables a cruising speed of over 200 m.p.h. to be attained also and after an allowance has been made for head winds and the operational delays referred to in manoeuvring in and out of airports, the time-tables can actually guarantee speeds of 200 m.p.h. in nearly all weathers. One such air liner which will be able to fulfil these conditions is the Clyde Clipper lifting-fuselage monoplane, a 14/20 passenger seater type the Scottish Aircraft and Engineering Company are now building at Wembley, on the outskirts of north London.

This will be able to give passengers on the home airways 200 m.p.h. air travel.

The giant flying boats now being designed for use by 1940 will also be able to assure travel at this speed.

That will get us most of the way towards this goal. If 4,000 miles are to be flown per day on an air route, obviously the aircraft will keep going day and night for 20 hours out of 24. But this will be quite practicable. All experience shows that short stages of 500 miles at a time are desirable, for then the air liner or flying boat can descend to re-fuel without carrying too heavy a fuel load at the expense of passengers, International mails or freight.

Night Flying

All the Empire routes can be served by such short stages, except the ocean crossings, including the Atlantic, the Pacific, and the Tasman Sea between Australia and New Zealand.

The routes to India, the Cape, Singapore and Australia are to-day served by just such short stages as these. Night flying equipment is being laid down at them all. When this is completed, the air passenger will be able to fly by night as well as by day.

He will be able to stay in the air for 20 hours out of 24 and eight well-organised half-hour stops for fuelling, etc., will be all the time needed in harbours. At 200 m.p.h. he will thus cover 4,000 miles in a day.

Australia – 3 Days

By 1940 we shall see this goal attained and the startling results which will be seen can be gauged when we consider finally the times which it will take to reach various Empire destinations from England. Here are some of them.

India, which is about 5,000 miles away, will be reached in 30 hours. South Africa, which is a flight of about 8,000 miles, divided into some 26 stopping places on the Empire route, will be reached in 48 hours.

South American towns, which are 7,000 miles from London, will be reached in a weekend.

And Sydney and Melbourne, 12,000 miles from home, will be reached in three days when we travel 4,000 miles per day.

Thus the racing times set up by the high-speed monoplane in the MacRobertson Races of 1934 will become the standard commercial flights of 1940.

Comfort

Nor will the passengers be rushed in discomfort breathlessly from one end of the world to the other, for this would never do.

They will fly in luxurious lounges in the giant aircraft, which will be twice the size and weight of the 40,500 lbs. Empire types. And at night they will sleep soundly and comfortably in berths which will compare well with first-class ocean travel. Speed for the air passenger is thus no idle dream.

On the contrary, he is going to demand it and once it is placed within his reach, the volume of air travel will grow at a pace which will amaze the most optimistic of air line operators and the most enthusiastic among those of us who want to see the Empire girded with a chain of high-speed aeroplanes.

WHAT IT FEELS LIKE TO FLY AT 400 M.P.H.
– AND "BLACK-OUT"
By Victor Burnett, 1937

I have just flown at more than 400 miles an hour. No other newspaperman has ever reached this speed. The world's speed record is 440 m.p.h.

It was at once the most exhilarating and terrifying experience I have ever had.

The speed itself, until I saw the clouds and the ground, felt no different from any other speed I have flown at.

But the sudden feeling of crushing weight when the machine banked round in a turn at 300 m.p.h. was sheer nightmare horror.

I was watching the altimeter as we took off.

As I looked I received the first impression of something unusual. The needle was racing round the dial like the seconds hand of a clock, checking off thousands of feet of height almost in instants.

Down below, as I turned my head I saw the ground visibly shrinking. A great hangar contracted as I looked at it. No other airplane I had ever flown climbed like this.

There was a white, pasty flash past the wings as we rocketed through a cloud layer and out into the sunlight of the upper air. Still we climbed – ten, fifteen thousand feet. Then we levelled out.

The throttle moved forward. Ahead of me the great supercharged engine roared into a scream. A touch on the control column and the nose dropped just a fraction below the horizon. We began a shallow dive.

I watched the speed indicator. The sight was incredible. From 250 it moved on to 290, then 300 – 320 – 350 – 380. I couldn't believe it. Still the needle swept on – 390 – 400.

I looked out.

The cloud layer was rushing up at us.

As I looked it smashed towards us, broke, became a flash of white oblivion – and then a bank of grey cloud far above our heads.

Earth lay below instead of cloud.

The contracting process was reversed. Before my eyes the ground grew ever larger. The altimeter needle spun round the other way, decreasing its height instead of increasing it.

We checked the speed and pulled out of the dive; once more we zoomed through the clouds.

Then the horror began. The monoplane was put into a steep, high-speed turn.

As it started I felt my entire body begin to grow heavier. Some gigantic, invisible force seemed to be pushing me down into my seat, not only from outside me, but from within. Breathing became difficult.

My power of thought began to go. I couldn't reason. A feeling of intense physical distress started.

I couldn't move my head. I was pinioned. The sun swam into my vision. It didn't blind me, but moved across the sky like a cold, white globe. The horror increased. Incoherent thoughts chased themselves through my brain.

And then the sun began to flicker in a dreary grey light.

Faster it flickered, and faster into a whirling dance that broke it up into solid pieces of darkness, a darkness that suddenly enveloped everything.

I had blacked out. My weight had increased so much that my heart could no longer pump blood to my brain.

Suddenly I could see again, we were coming

The most prized piece of silverplate? This impressive trophy was presented by Pierre II Roi of Yugoslavia in 1938 for competition by *model* aeroplanes! The first successful flight by a clockwork-powered model aeroplane took place in around 1857.

out of the turn. Darkness vanished. The grey flicker steadied.

But I had lost all sense of perception. I did not know whether the machine was on its back or right way up. I did not care. Out on one side I could see the earth through broken clouds. On the other I could see the sky.

In that turn, my weight had increased from twelve stone to thirty-six stone through the force of acceleration.

The force that makes this weight increase is called " G" by scientists. We went up to three

"G" – three times gravity. This multiplies your weight by three.

The force is caused through acceleration. Very strong men have stood a force of nine "G" and lived – but this is rare. A fit man can go up to six – which means that if normally he weighs twelve stone, he weighs seventy-two stone under the force.

The throttle was cut. We came in to land. I lost all judgment of speeds below 150 miles an hour. The landing seemed slow. I slid back the cabin cover and stepped out – to think.

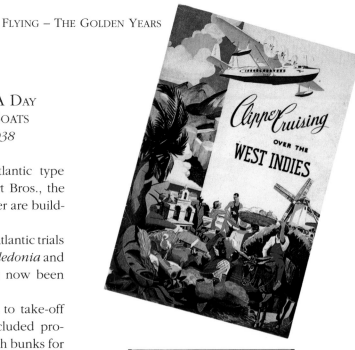

A Sikorsky S-42 flying the 7,777 miles of the "Lindbergh Circle". In the 30s it was realised that night sleepers were not the answer to long distance air travel, since it was difficult for passengers to sleep comfortably.

LONDON – NEW YORK IN A DAY
ENGLAND'S NEW FLYING BOATS
By William Courtenay, 1938

First details of the three new Atlantic type passenger flying boats which Short Bros., the famous aircraft builders of Rochester are building, may now be revealed.

Following the highly successful Atlantic trials of the Short Empire type boats, *Caledonia* and *Cambria* three larger vessels have now been laid down.

The Empire type was designed to take-off fully loaded at 40,500 lb. This included provision for 24 passengers by day, with bunks for 16 by night baggage; mails and freight, and a crew of five; up to 5 tons of payload, in fact, was called for in the design. Short Bros. have been highly successful in fulfilling this requirement.

The Empire type has been able to cruise at 165 m.p.h, which has nearly doubled the speeds at which Imperial Airways previously operated the Empire routes. During 1937, a fleet of 25 of these boats was brought to birth, a truly remarkable and highly creditable performance.

Of these, two were specially strengthened for the Atlantic experimental services.

It was realised, of course, that the 40,500-lb. boat could not provide fuel for the four engines and carry a pay-load across 2,000 miles of open ocean, non-stop as well.

Thus, both *Caledonia* and *Cambria* were selected for special treatment. They were strengthened to load up to 45,000 lbs. and were given Certificates of Airworthiness at that figure.

It is interesting to note that the great fuel loads were carried in the wings only, and that there was plenty of room for the normal complement of 24 passengers. There was not the weight available to carry them once the flying boats were loaded for Atlantic flights.

The empty weight of the Empire type flying boat, including hull, engines instruments, etc., is 24,650 lbs.

Caledonia and *Cambria* had to carry some 2,320 gallons of petrol each trip. This gave the boats a range of about 3,500 miles in calm air. It mean that if they had to fight a 40 m.p.h head wind between the Empire air bases at Loynes,

Ireland, and Botwood, Newfoundland, they would have enough fuel for that 1,993 miles crossing and still land with a reserve.

In practice, these boats were throttled back to 150 m.p.h. to conserve fuel and extend range. If a 40 m.p.h. constant head wind had been experienced, the progress pace over the Atlantic would have been reduced to 110 m.p.h.

The 2,000-mile crossing would, in such circumstances, have taken 18 hours. Since the four Bristol Pegasus 920 h.p. radial air-cooled engines consume about 110 gallons of fuel per hour between them, they carried about a 20 hours' supply (2,320 gallons). Thus, even in the most disadvantageous of conditions, there would always have been a two hours' fuel supply left in reserve on landing.

The 2,320 gallons of petrol, with the necessary quantity of lubricating oil, weighed some 18,750 lbs. This figure, with the empty weight of the flying boat, totals 43,400 lbs. If 800 lbs. be added for the crew of four, the total rises to 44,200 lbs. This left only some 800 lbs. out of the upper limit of 45,000 lbs. at the take-off for any payload. Thus, *Caledonia*, in which Capt. A.. S. Wilcockson completed six satisfactory crossings of the Atlantic, and *Cambria*, which Capt. G. J. Powell with equal brilliance commanded on four such trips, could carry air mail up to

Flying cruises
around South
America 1940. The
capable and
shapely Boeing-
built Clippers of
Pan American were
the principal rivals
to the Short flying
boats.

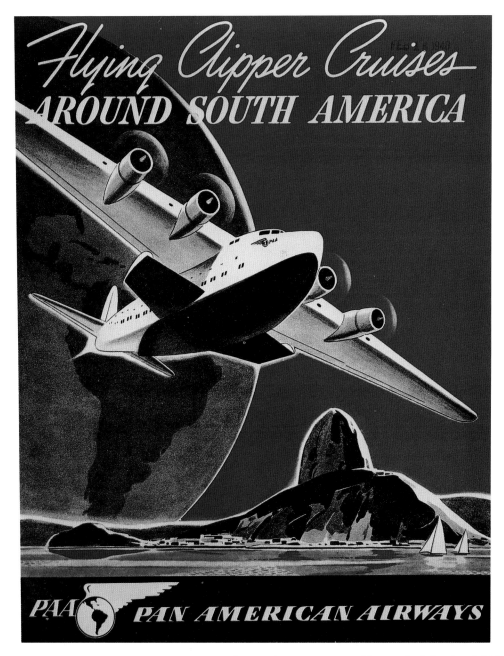

about 800 lbs. or about four passengers with a little baggage.

The experience of the Atlantic crossings of these two specially strengthened Empire type boats has paved the way for the larger boats which these figures show are so necessary before any appreciable payload can be carried to America by air.

The basic principle remains as indeed it must and will in the design of all the flying boats which Imperial Airways use on the North Atlantic; that is that the vessel must be able in the first place to carry sufficient fuel for the 2,000-mile ocean crossing against a constant 40-m.p.h. head wind. This wise provision guards against all risks of a forced descent through fuel shortage, provided, of course, pilots do not lose their way; either through a navigational error or as a result of flying conditions.

It means, in effect, that all flying boats crossing the Atlantic and all landplanes, too, will always carry sufficient fuel and oil for a range of about 3,500 miles in calm air, thus guarding against the risk of running short of fuel in adverse conditions.

Stationery was provided for the fortunate passengers on the Brazilian leg of their journey by the carrier PANAIR. Passengers are seen here deplaning from a Commodore flying boat.

M.P.H. Average

Starting with this formula, Short Bros. decided to push the total all-up weight of the new Atlantic boats they are now building to some 70,000 lbs.

Bigger boats depend upon bigger engine output. Here the Bristol Aeroplane Company once more comes to the rescue.

The new Hercules sleeve-valve radial air-cooled engine will be used. These will develop 1,380 h.p. at the take-off. Four of them mounted along the leading edge of the monoplane wing – two on either side of the hull – will produce a total of 5,520 h.p. contrasted with 3,480 h.p. of the four Pegasus types. Instead of cruising at 165 m.p.h., the new 70,000 lb. boats will cruise at about 181 m.p.h. at 5,000ft. This will be a very useful reserve against head winds.

In practice, during the summer months, when Botwood is free from ice and when the flying boat will be the normal transport vehicle for the Atlantic air route, winds will not average more than 30 m.p.h. This means that progress pace over the water will not fall below an average of 150 m.p.h. for the ocean crossing.

Newfoundland will be reached from Ireland in 13 to 14 hours at the most. In the reverse direction, even where such winds do not aid the pilot, the crossing should not average more than 11 hours, for the full advantage of 180 m.p.h. cruising speed can be assured. Where an average 30 m.p.h. following wind is experienced the flying boat will bowl along at 210 m.p.h. and will cross the 2,000 miles of ocean in the remarkable fast time of about 9 hours.

Similar contrasts in schedules were put up by Capt. Wilcockson and Capt. Powell this summer, and by Capt. Grey, the skipper of the Pan-American Sikorsky Clipper ship, though not, of course, at the same high speeds.

The structure weight of the new 70,000 lb. boats will absorb 36,000 lbs. This will leave some 34,000 lbs. for fuel and oil; pilots and crew; passengers and baggage; mails and freight, food and water.

The fuel supply will be approximately 3,350 gallons. With oil, it will weigh about 28,000 lbs. These figures account for some 64,000 lbs. About 6,000 lbs. is left over for crew and payload.

A crew of five at 200 lbs. each, including their kit, will account for 1,000 lbs. of this. The other 5,000 lbs. may be allotted to air mails and a few passengers.

Seating for 24

The Atlantic type is to have seats for 24 passengers, and the weight of the cabin fittings, seats, furnishings, sound-proofing, etc., is included in the empty weight figure of 36,000 lbs. already given.

If the 5,000 lbs. available for pay-load were utilised for passengers and if 220 lbs. be allotted to each (including baggage) then some 20 could be carried (4,440 lbs.) and there would be 660 lbs left over for rations.

In practice, next summer, however, it will be found that these three Atlantic boats will be used partly to carry the first experimental air mail loads between England, Ireland, Newfoundland, Canada and New York, and a few privileged passengers. These will not be fare-paying passengers, nor will the route be open to

Left:

Pan American show off their Havana-Nassau route, in 1935. The amphibian is another S-42 Sikorsky, which had replaced the S-40 (rather ungenerously described as a "collection of spare parts flying in formation").

Aeromarine Service, circa 1922. The U.S. was, in comparison with Europe, a late starter in air transport but was to achieve a powerful position domestically in little over a decade and a half.

the public in 1938. They will be officials of the Air Ministry, of Imperial Airways, and of the various firms who have constructed the aircraft, engines instruments, and so on. There will be traffic staff to train and pilots and crews to learn the demanding and exacting job of operating an Atlantic air service.

Ready by June

The first of these three Atlantic type flying boats is expected to be ready for delivery from Short Bros. to Imperial Airways in June, 1938. The other two are certain to follow in quick succession.

We shall, I predict, see the first air mail loads carried by these boats to America, apart from what the Mayo Composite Seaplane may do.

If air mail loads are restricted to a ton (2,240 lbs.) there will still be room for up to a dozen official passengers.

Even when head winds are blowing at their strongest intensity, we should see schedules which will bring London and New York within less than 24 hours of each other.

Top Right:
SCADTA (later Avianca) publicity of 1931, showing the huge German seaplane, the Dornier Wal *Columbia.* After World War II, the flying boat fell out of favour and rarely seen.

Coast to coast - the aeroplanes are a Ford Tri-Motor, considered in the late 1920s to be the last word in modern technology, and an all-metal, eight-seater Hamilton seaplane.

This cutaway reveals the interior of the "Hythe" flying boat. The China Tea Clippers of their day, flying boats evoke nostalgia even amongst those too young to have known them.

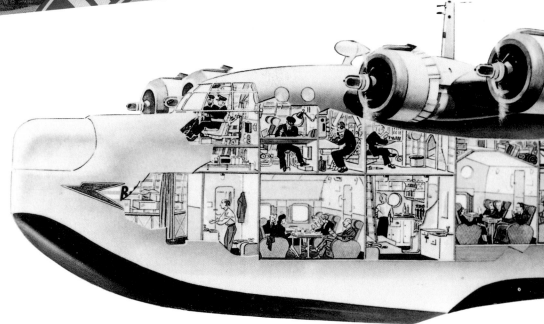

128

Right:
Clipper flying
vessels circle the
globe and compli-
ment the stylised
Douglas DC-3,
which, with its
forerunner the DC-
2, was one of the
most successful
airliners in history.

Left:
Colonial Western
Airlines advertis-
ing, from 1928.
Instead of paying to
watch aeroplanes
fly, the public
began, by the end
of the decade, to
pay to fly in them.

BRITAINS BIGGEST
1938

The introduction of the "Ensign" Air-liners, the first of which has recently undergone successful initial trials, marks a further step forward in the progress of British Civil Aviation., the new machines will not only be the largest in regular service in the world, but probably be the fastest of their size.

Altogether, reckoning additions to the Company's fleet of marine aircraft, Imperial Airways now have in operation or construction 86 big multi-engined aircraft.

Trials

In this connection, and as some indication of the progress made during the past fourteen years, it may be mentioned that when the Company first began flying in 1924 its entire fleet did not total more than 15 single- and twin-engined aircraft.

The latest addition to the Company's increasing fleet is the "E" class liner, the first of which has recently under-gone satisfactory preliminary tests, and fourteen of which are actually scheduled for construction at a cost of some £750,000.

The initial flight proved entirely successful from a technical viewpoint, and this first "Ensign" air-liner will now be carrying out further manufacturers' trials, after which it will pass into the hands of the Air Ministry for official tests before coming into regular service on the Imperial Airways' routes.

Speed and Power Reserve

Known to the constructors as the W. 27, and the largest aircraft in regular operation in the world, they will take their place in Imperial Airways fleet as completed, a number being of a "European" type to be used on Imperial Airways' continental routes whilst the others will be of an "Empire" type and will be specially equipped to work the Empire land-plane services which are to be operated in conjunction with the flying-boat services.

Each of the new air-liners will be equipped with four Armstrong Siddeley "Tiger IX" medium super-charged engines built into the lead-ing edge of the wings and fitted with de Havilland controllable pitch propellers.

These four engines will provide a total of no less than 3,400 horse-power, giving ample power reserve and enabling the air-liner to maintain height with full load at 12,500 feet on three engines and at 4,000 feet on two engines only.

It is anticipated that this new fleet will prove to be the fastest of its size in the world. A feature of the design is the remarkable streamline form which has enabled the constructors to combine speed with size. A top speed of more than 200 miles an hour is expected.

Constructional Details

The fuel tanks are built into the wings and the tankage will be sufficient to give the aircraft a wide range making it possible, with slight adjustments of load, to fly 1,000 miles non-stop against a headwind of 40 miles an hour. The new airliner is a high-wing cantilever monoplane of all-metal construction, the fuselage being an oval monocque structure completely covered with metal sheets of light alloy presenting a smooth outer surface. Technically, one of the features of the design is the form of construction used in the wing. This is tapered in plan form and thickness and is built on a single, rectangular box-spar of corrugated light-alloy sheet, which is the subject of an Armstrong Whitworth patent.

Colossal Undercarriage

Split trailing edge flaps are fitted, of a type, which, in effect, increase the wing area, being used for increasing the lift at take-off and also increasing drag, so consequently reducing the speed at landing.

The undercarriage – the largest in the world – is retractable, despite its colossal size, and has two single wheels each of which requires a tyre 6ft. 3ins. in diameter and 2ft. 2ins. wide. No tyre of these dimensions has ever ordinarily been manufactured and special tyres are to be constructed by the Dunlop Rubber Company. The retracting mechanism is hydraulically operated. The rear strut of each leg folds and the wheels travel backwards and upwards into the engine fairings behind the main 'plane spars.

Elimination of Noise

The question of eliminating vibration and noise, an important factor in the construction of air-liners, has been the subject of intensive research by experts engaged on the construction of the new air-liners.

Vibrationary noise is frequently transmitted from the engines to the hull through the wings. This is obviated on the new aircraft by insulating the engines from the wings with patent flexible engine mountings.

The problem of extraneous noises has been dealt with in several ways. One prolific cause of noise in aircraft is the high speed of the tips of the propeller-blades and in the new aircraft this is overcome by arrangements to operate the propellers at comparatively low speeds.

New methods of sound proofing are employed. Special bulkheads, which prevent humming are fitted, and specially thickened window glass also assists in keeping the saloons free from extraneous noise. An additional aid to silence will be the placing of the passenger saloons away from that part of the fuselage in line with the engines.

The "European" type air-liner will be able to carry up to 42 passengers. Modifications will be made to the Empire type owing to the necessity of special equipment for journeys of long duration in tropical climates and the carriage of larger loads of mails, 27 passengers will be carried on day flights, while, for night journeys, sleeping berths, quickly dismantled, will be provided for 20.

The passenger chairs have been designed by experts of Imperial Airways after more than two years of research. These chairs can be adjusted to any position from the almost vertical to the almost horizontal by the passenger while actually seated. They weigh only 19 pounds – the lightest and yet one of the most comfortable lounge chairs ever constructed.

Built for Comfort

Heating and ventilation are under a system of control developed by Sir W. G. Armstrong Whitworth Aircraft. Fresh, clean air is drawn in around a steam heater operated from the engine exhausts and this will be circulated evenly through all the passenger saloons, affording a constant supply of air untainted by engine fumes at an equable temperature.

The interior layout will include several passenger saloons as well as a promenade deck.

Besides the saloons, there will be two separate lavatories, a completely equipped kitchen and well-stocked bar, mail and freight holds and even a ship's office. This office will be used by a ship's clerk who will have the duty of checking freight and mail cargoes during flight.

From the kitchen, in accordance with Imperial Airways' long-standing practice on their larger aircraft, it will be possible to serve seven-course dinners as well as five-course lunch and snacks and drinks of all descriptions. Truly air travel de-luxe!

The Control Room will be situated in the extreme nose of the fuselage and the Commander and First Officer will have side-by-side dual control with separate columns and hand wheels and parallel motion rudder bars. They will have at their disposal an Automatic Pilot and every modern piloting and navigational aid that has proved efficient under extensive test

In the Control Room, too, will be a wireless operator who, with a short and long-wave receiver and transmitter and direction-finding apparatus, will be able to keep in constant touch with ground stations; the other two members of the crew of five will both be stewards who will cater for the comfort of passengers.

New Records?

The design of these air-liners is the natural outcome of ordered and economic air progress and they are confidently expected to set new records for size and luxury, combined with high operational speeds.

A sign painter at work, at Short Bros, Rochester, Kent. During World War I, the labour force was sparse and it was estimated that the engineering trades lost one in five of their pre-war male workers.

SPEEDING-UP THE AUSTRALIAN MAIL
1938

"You must run while you can, fight when you can no longer run, and then throw the Mails overboard when fighting will no longer avail."

That, in a nutshell, was how the Empire Mail was handled in the early days of our overseas Dominions! The paragraph quoted was amongst the official instructions to the commanders of private vessels which, about the year of the battle of Trafalgar, 1805, were responsible for carrying the few letters and packages which constituted the Empire Mail.

No better indication of the rigours of their duties could be found than the scale of pensions awarded for injuries received in the Packet Service, as it was called.

This scale included £8 a year for every arm or leg amputated above the elbow or knee; £4 a year for the loss of the sight of one eye; £12 for the sight of both eyes; while the official communique concluded with the words " ... and according to these rates we consider also how much the hurts affect the body and make the allowances accordingly".

Obviously, the carrying of the Mail in those days was no sinecure, but rather an adventure fraught with the most desperate dangers!

In the year 1798, Mr. Bourne, the Assistant Inspector of Dead Letters, tried – in vain – to establish a Ship's Letter Office. His words were somewhat censorious: "The Postmaster-General does not possess the means sufficiently to secure and facilitate the conveyance of all correspondence now carried by private ships. The established medium for the conveyance of letters is so evidently defective as to render the mode of sending them by private vessels and private persons indispensable".

Years After

Nevertheless, it was not until 1837 that the first contract was granted by His Majesty's Government, to the Peninsular and Oriental Steamship Company, and it was not until fifteen years later that the Mail Steamship *Chrisan* left England for Australia carrying the first Mail between the two

countries; and with this venture began the story of the regular Australian Mail, which we of the present generation have seen developed to an extent not then dreamed of.

Thus, on August 3rd, 1852, the *Chrisan* arrived in Sydney, to herald a new era in the transport of Mails between England and Australia. Writing of this event, the *Sydney Morning Herald* said in a triumphant tone: "To England, as well as ourselves, steam communication by sea is of unspeakable importance. . . The immediate effect will be to reduce the distance between us and England, by at least one-half . . . we must congratulate Australia upon the auspicious era for which she has long been sighing, but which is now illuminating her horizon with the brightest dawn of promise".

Thereafter, for many years, the story is one of the vision of the owners and the courage and skill of the officers and men of the British Mercantile Marine, who have since carried the

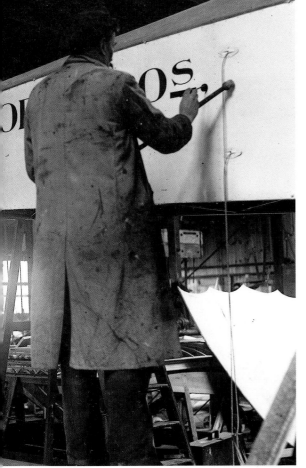

Bermuda by air - a joint service by Imperial Airways (Bermuda) and Pan American Airways began in June 1937 and employed a Short S-23 (*RMA Cavalier*) and an S-42 (*Clipper*).

The big S-42 gave sterling service on the run from Miami to Rio and Buenos Aires before the near-eclipse of boat and float planes.

135

Australian Mail with a regularity and devotion to duty which at once provides an inspiration and a tradition for the air services of to-day to emulate – no mean task. Nor must the services of the cable and wireless system be forgotten, for they have, and are, conferring immeasurable benefits to Australia.

The First Steps

Just after the close of the World War, Capt. Ross Smith, D.F.C., with Major-General W. G. H. Salmond, D.S.O., commanding the Royal Air Force in the Far East, and Brigadier-General A. E. Borton and two mechanics, began the first flight from Heliopolis to Delhi in a Handley-Page twin-engined bomber. Following upon this successful flight, Capt. Ross Smith and Brigadier-General Borton began in the spring of 1919, a "grand survey" of the air route between India and Australia, in the *S.S. Sphinx* and *Mino* of the Royal Indian Marine.

A new era in the transport of the Australian Mail had begun, and the first links in the chain of accomplished facts were being forged.

In October, 1919, an Advisory Committee on Civil Aviation, under the Chairmanship of Lord Weir, recommended the establishment of certain "main trunk lines connecting Canada, Newfoundland, South Africa, Australia and New Zealand to the United Kingdom by air." Two days later, the Controller-General of Civil Aviation announced that the Cairo-Karachi route had been opened for military purposes and would be available for civil traffic at an early date. He also added in this, his first public report, that a full reconnaissance of the route from London to Australia had also been completed.

On the 11th December, 1919, Captain Ross Smith and his companions, in a twin-engined Vickers Vimy biplane, accomplished the first flight from Great Britain to Australia. They covered the distance of 11,294 miles in just under 28 days, winning the prize of £10,000 offered by the Australian Government.

The West Indies edition of *The Air Traveller*, with an artist's impression of a S-42 on the cover, from 1941. The late 1940's saw the rebirth of civilian air travel and the introduction of the world's first gas-turbine airliners.

GO BY
PRIVATE
AEROPLANE

Perfect Comfort

IMPERIAL
AIRWAYS

Top Right:
Two "types" enjoy a cocktail in the pocket cartoon *In Perfect Comfort.* An anonymous British Member of Parliament wrote of the Handley Page H.P.42: "And the bar! From what I saw of the bottles behind the grille, to say nothing of the cups and saucers, the steward in attendance will be able to give a very efficient service."

Top Left:
CNAC - a Douglas Dolphin of the China National Aviation Corp., in 1936. Engineer Donald Douglas established a factory in California to build aeroplanes for the US Navy in the 1920s.

Flying the flag - another artist's interpretation of an S-42 Clipper.

137

Bill Boeing started his factory in California to build aircraft for Navy contracts. The enormous 314 pictured here in 1939 was analogous with the Short boats and flew on a regular trans-Atlantic air-route during World War II.

Organisation

Seven years were then to elapse before the next "landmark." In 1926, Mr. Alan Cobham reached Port Darwin from England in 36 days, flying a single-engined D.H.50 biplane.

Following upon the efforts of these pioneers came a period of organisation, and in the early part of 1931 the first official air mail from England to Australia left Croydon, being part of an arrangement between the Post Office, the Air Ministry, and Imperial Airways for the operation of two experimental flights in each direction between London and Australia. These flights were, in effect, an extension of the existing London-Karachi and Karachi-Delhi services.

In January, 1934, Qantas Empire Airways Ltd., formed to operate the England-Australia route in association with Imperial Airways, and in December of that year two tons of Mail load left England for the East, half a ton being destined for places beyond Singapore, mostly in

138

Australia and New Zealand. Among the letters were three addressed by the King, the Queen and the Prince of Wales to the Duke of Gloucester in Auckland. The mail left in the *Hengist.*

A day or two later a weekly London – Brisbane service was begun by Imperial Airways and Qantas Empire Airways, and a few weeks after Sir Philip Sassoon announced in the House of Commons a far-reaching and ambitious scheme for the development of the Empire Air Services.In emphasising that a further two years must elapse before the scheme would be in operation, Sir Philip Sassoon described the project as "the largest step forward which has yet been taken in the development of Empire Air communication".

Early in 1935, a weekly air service between London and Brisbane was opened for the carriage of passengers. In 1936, this was further extended to a twice-weekly service.

Then, in the same year, the introduction of the Imperial Airways Empire flying boats brought the plans for the development of the services within sight of completion.

As a prelude to the establishment of a flying boat service between England and Sydney, the Empire boat, with a crew of six, left Southampton Water for New Zealand.

She arrived at Auckland in twenty-three days, after an uneventful flight, and at last proof of efficiency and reliability was no longer wanting.

On July 28th, this year, the Empire Flying Boat *Clio* left Southampton carrying the first all-up Mail for Australia .

Now, every Thursday, Saturday, and Sunday the flying boats of Imperial Airways and of Qantas Empire Airways will carry all the first-class Mail between Australia and England.

Time has been reduced from months to days. Speed has once again benefited mankind. Behind these bald notes which record the history of the developments lies romance for the imaginative reader.

It is a far cry from the days of "four good, substantial and efficient steam vessels".

The Sikorsky S-40 - Igor Sikorsky had built an experimental helicopter as early as 1910, a form of transport for which he was later to become famous.

Rara avis - T.E.
Slot, engineer and
constructor,
standing in the
cockpit of the
Scheldemusch. Slot
was also responsi-
ble for the
Panderjager, a
twin-engined
aircraft that took
part in the Mel-
bourne air race of
1934, crewed by
Asjes, Pronk and
Geyssendorfer,
maestro of the air
and legendary KLM
pilot.

SPEED ROUND THE WORLD
By Prof. A.M. Low, 1937

When the North Atlantic passenger service is
opened with large flying boats carrying passengers, it will be possible to travel round the world
by ordinary air routes in about twenty days. The
only skill required will be juggling with time-
tables, and if anything is required to show how
the world has speeded up in the last sixty years,
you have only to consider this in relation to the
publication of Jules Verne's famous book, *Round
the World in Eighty Days.* When this appeared in
1874, it was considered a fairly vivid flight of
imagination and there were probably thousands
of people ready to wager that the book would
not "come true" in a good many years, if ever.

To-day an aeroplane that set out to fly round
the world could accomplish the journey in five
days at the equator. This would call for a speed
of only 200 m.p.h., and in the future may well
be done in two "hops." 12,000 miles, for technical reasons, is believed to be about the limit for
a non-stop flight by an aeroplane fitted with
engines of the type used to-day, but a study of

the history of speed shows the dangers of giving
limits of any kind.

Nothing very practical is accomplished by
speeding round the world, unless you wish for
first-hand proof that the world is indeed round,
and, according to the "Flat Earth" Societies, even
this evidence is not convincing. Nevertheless,
racing round the world has never failed to
attract men since the feat was first accomplished
by Sir Francis Drake. Actually, Drake was not
the first man to travel round the world. Magellan's
expedition had done it more than fifty years
before, but Magellan himself was killed in the
Philippines with only half the journey completed, and only one of his five boats returned
to Spain.

To-day you can do the journey comfortably
at an average speed of 150 m.p.h. Magellan's
ships took three years, all but a few days. The
Pacific, now crossed regularly by "China Clippers" in the course of a day or two took
Magellan's men 100 days.

Drake's time took even longer. He set out in
December, 1577, and the Golden Hind did not
appear off the English coast again until three

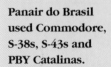

years and four months later. Drake however was not out for a speed record; he turned aside more than once for a spell of exploring and plundering. His journey was, of course, of tremendous importance, quite regardless of the time taken.

Improvements in the construction of ships enabled the time taken for travelling round the world to be steadily reduced, but it is safe to say that less than twelve months would have been good going at the end of the 18th century – less than 150 years ago. Men still depended upon the wind to give them speed over the water and upon horses to carry them over the land.

The World Shrinks

After the completion of the first of the great trans-continental railways and the building of steam-ships that were reliable, and, compared with sailing ships, reasonably fast, the world became much smaller. About fifteen years after Jules Verne wrote *Round the World in Eighty Days*, the world was actually circumnavigated in 72 days, and it is worth noting that the pioneer was a woman! Miss Nellie Bly, making full use of every facility of transport available, caused quite a sensation with her record journey.

After that, however, the record came tumbling down. It became chiefly a matter of studying time-tables, for individual methods of travel by aeroplane and motor car were not in existence. If you wanted to speed round the world, you had to speed in the company of others, unless you were prepared to spend very large sums. The record for the round trip by "standard" means of transport was roughly then down to 60 days immediately on the opening of the Trans-Siberia railway. If aeroplanes and racing cars are

Panair do Brasil used Commodore, S-38s, S-43s and PBY Catalinas.

One candidate for the airline's attention, when it was introduced in 1934, was the Lockheed Electra, a most successful smaller type of transport aeroplane.

Three De Havilland DH88 Comet racing monoplanes were built for the MacRobertson air race from Mildenhall, England, to Melbourne, Australia, in 1934. Tom Campbell-Black clinched victory at Laverton Airfield, Melbourne, with C.W.A. Scott. The plane, successfully restored, survives today.

barred, it is difficult to beat this time even to-day, for neither express trains nor liners have very appreciably increased their speed in the last 30 years.

The Cost of Speed

Racing round the world became quite a sport and a fairly expensive one. I have a record that one "competitor" accomplished the feat in 36 days at a cost of about £170, which seems cheap in view of the fact that he engaged special transport in certain places. It is difficult to say what the actual "record" is, for so much depends upon the rules. If competitors are allowed to engage special trains or motor cars, thirty days should be possible. Using the, then, available air transport, two travellers went round the world in 28 days in 1926, and still using standard means of transport, the journey was accomplished in 24 days in 1930. This is an average of 1,000 miles a day, not a very high average speed, but it must be remembered that it is 24,000 miles round the equator as the crow flies and not as the steamship and railway companies take you.

After several attempts which ended in failure, the first round-the-world flight was made by four American 'planes in 1924, but the time taken did not suggest we had advanced very far from the days of Drake – 174 days. Of course, only a proportion of these were spent in the air. In 1929, the *Graf Zeppelin*, just retired, made the trip in 21 days, of which 13 were spent in the air. The record came down with a jump two years later when Wiley Post and Gatty made it 9 days, and in 1933, Wiley Post made a remarkable solo flight in 7 days 18 hours. From the point of view of physical endurance alone it would be difficult to beat this record.

I must point out here that all these flights were not made round the world at the equator, but in northern latitudes, so that the distance was smaller. If a "round-the-world" record is to be established, some rules will have to be made about the distance covered. Obviously, the further from the equator the less the mileage to get back to where you started from. As a polar explorer once pointed out you can "go round the world" at the North Pole in about five minutes!

When Time Stands Still

There is a certain fascination about round-the-world flying, even if it has no obviously practical value. The most interesting trip round the world will be that accomplished at a speed of 900 m.p.h. This is the speed at which the earth rotates and thus it would be possible for time – as shown by our watches – to stand still during the flight. If you started at midnight, it would be midnight in every country over which you passed and you would arrive back at midnight – on the next day. This speed on a trip round the world would make it possible to travel all the way by night or day as you chose.

Nine hundred miles an hour may seem a long way off, but to make the trip entirely in daylight in northerly latitudes would require a speed not so very much greater than that already attained. And remember that Jules Verne thought he was being bold in talking of *Round the World in Eighty Days*!

> Our descendants will certainly attempt journeys to other members of the Solar system. . . . By 2030 the first preparations for the first attempt to reach Mars may perhaps be under consideration. The hardy individuals who form the personnel of the expedition will be sent forth in a machine propelled like a rocket.
>
> LORD BIRKENHEAD (1930)

GOLD MEDAL ESSAY (AIR)

The subject of the gold medal essay of the Royal United Service Institution for 1938 is: "Discuss the influence which modern air forces may exert on British strategy in a major European war in which Great Britain is involved; and suggest what higher control organisation is desirable in order to coordinate the operations of the three services."

> Scientific investigation into the possibilities [of jet propulsion] has given no indication that this method can be a serious competitor to the airscrew-engine combination.
>
> THE BRITISH UNDER-SECRETARY OF STATE FOR AIR (1934)

25 JAHRE SCHWEIZER LUFTWAFFE

MILITÄR FLUGTAGE 1939 DÜBENDORF 2/3. SEPT. ODER 9/10. SEPT.

The spur of war - the message in this composition is striking and clear. At the close of play in 1939, the speed record, standing at 469.12 mph, was held by a German Messerschmitt Bf 109R.

143

ACKNOWLEDGEMENTS

All efforts have been made to contact the copyright holders of any material in this book that may be in copyright, but Morgan Samuel Editions would be grateful to receive any notice of any copyright material that may have been overlooked.

Morgan Samuel Editions would like to express their gratitude to the following individuals and organisations who have supplied the illustrations in this book:

Opposite title page: Illustrated London News; p10: Khachadourian Gallery; pp12/13/14/15: Mary Anne Roberts; p15 *top left*: London Borough of Sutton Heritage Service; pp16/17/18/19: Khachadourian Gallery; p20: Royal Aeronautical Society; p21: Mary Anne Roberts; pp22/23: Brooklands Museum; p24 *top*: Mary Anne Roberts; p24 bottom Royal Aeronautical Society; p25: Brooklands Museum; pp26/27: Brooklands Museum; pp28/29 *top*: Rupert Prior; pp28/29 others: Mary Anne Roberts; p30: Brooklands Museum; p31: Mary Anne Roberts; pp32/33: Brooklands Museum; p33 *bottom* Mary Anne Roberts; pp34/35: Brooklands Museum; p36: Khachadourian Gallery; p37: Brooklands Museum; pp38/39/40/41: Brooklands Museum; pp42/43 *top*: Mary Anne Roberts; p42/43 *bottom*: Royal Aeronautical Society; p43 *top*: Brooklands Museum; p43 *bottom*: Khachadourian Gallery; pp44/45/46/47: Adrian Meredith Photography; pp48/49: Khachadourian Gallery; p50 *top*: Courtesy Don Thomas; p50 *bottom*: London Borough of Sutton Heritage Service; p51/52: Khachadourian Gallery; p54 *top*: Royal Aeronautical Society; pp54/55: Brooklands Museum; p55: Courtesy Don Thomas; pp56/57 *middle* Brooklands Museum; pp56/57 *bottom*: John Frost; p57: Khachadourian Gallery; p59 *top*: Royal Aeronautical Society; p59 *bottom*: Mary Anne Roberts; p60 *top left*: Khachadourian Gallery; pp60/61 *others*: Mary Anne Roberts; pp62/63: Brooklands Museum; p64: Khachadourian Gallery; p65: Courtesy Don Thomas; p66: Brooklands Museum; p67: Khachadourian Gallery; pp68/69: Rupert Prior; p69: Brooklands Museum; p70: Khachadourian Gallery; p71: Courtesy Don Thomas; pp72/73 *bottom*: London Borough of Sutton Heritage Service; pp73/74/75: Khachadourian Gallery; p76: Austin J Brown; p77/78: Khachadourian Gallery; p80: Royal Aeronautical Society; p81: Illustrated London News; p82 top: Khachadourian Gallery; p82 *bottom*: Courtesy Don Thomas; pp82/83: Mary Anne Roberts; pp94/85: Rupert Prior; pp86/87: Illustrated London News; p88: Khachadourian Gallery; p89: Mary Anne Roberts; p90 *top*: Khachadourian Gallery; p90 *bottom*: Courtesy Don Thomas; p91: Khachadourian Gallery; p92: Adrian Meredith Photography; p93: Courtesy Don Thomas; pp94/95: Khachadourian Gallery; p96: Illustrated London News; p98 *top*: Adrian Meredith Photography; p98 *bottom*: Mary Anne Roberts; p99 *top*: Courtesy Don Thomas; pp100/101/102/103: Courtesy Don Thomas; p104 *bottom*: Adrian Meredith Photography; p105 top: Adrian Meredith Photography; p105 *bottom*: London Borough of Sutton Heritage Service; p106: Khachadourian Gallery; p107: Courtesy Don Thomas; pp108/109: Illustrated London News; p110/111 *top*: Mary Anne Roberts; p110/111 *bottom*: Royal Aeronautical Society; pp111/112/113/114: Courtesy Don Thomas; p115 *bottom*: Royal Aeronautical Society; pp116/117: Courtesy Don Thomas; p118 *left*: London Borough of Sutton Heritage Service; p118 *right*: Brooklands Museum; p119: Illustrated London News; pp120/121 *main picture*: Adrian Meredith Photography; pp120/121 *others*: Brooklands Museum; p122: Khachadourian Gallery; p123 *left*: Khachadourian Gallery; p123 *right*: Courtesy Don Thomas; p124: Courtesy Don Thomas; pp125/126: Khachadourian Gallery; p127: Courtesy Don Thomas; pp128/129 *main picture*: Adrian Meredith Photography; pp128/129 *others*: Courtesy Don Thomas; p131: Mary Anne Roberts; pp132/133: Courtesy Don Thomas; pp134/135 *main picture*: Hulton Deutsch Collection; p135: Courtesy Don Thomas; pp136/137: Courtesy Don Thomas; p137 *middle right*: Adrian Meredith Photography; pp138/139: Courtesy Don Thomas; p140: Rupert Prior; p141 *bottom*: Royal Aeronautical Society; p141 *others*: Courtesy Don Thomas; p143: Khachadourian Gallery.

Editorial – Dr Jenny Sutcliffe & Cheryl Jacob
Design – Ran Barnes and Roger Abraham at The Creative Space
Original photography – Dick Cliff-Atkins
Production – Peter Price
Publisher – Nigel Perryman